A POST-WAR HALF CENTURY

A POST-WAR HALF CENTURY

CHRISTMAS LETTERS 1962-2011 EBERHARD GEORGE WEDELL & ROSEMARIE WEDELL

The Memoir Club

© Eberhard George Wedell 2012

First published in 2012 by
The Memoir Club
Arya House
Langley Park
Durham
DH7 9XE
Tel: 0191 373 5660
Email: memoirclub@msn.com

ISBN: 978-1-84104-545-0

Printed by Xpresslitho, Washington, Tyne & Wear

For Martin and Janet, his wife
Crispin,
Philip and Freda, his wife
and Rebecca and Shulamit, her partner.

Contents

List of Illustrations

Foreword

The rationale of this book derives from my intention to collect some autobiographical material. I collected chapter headings and developed some areas. Then I discovered that Rosemarie's and my joint Christmas letters had been preserved over half a century. They reflect quite interestingly our experiences and our concerns over much of the latter half of the twentieth century and the first decade of the twenty-first. So it seems a pity not to use them, and to link them with brief explanatory passages, as seen from the summer of 2012.

This will, I think, give a reasonably intelligent account of the last fifty years of our lives, and reach back in some respects to the previous forty years: 1920-1960. It is not comprehensive, and I keep open the possibility of recounting other areas of our experience. These might include a fuller treatment of such matters as the Student Christian Movement, the Chantry Group, the Wyndham Place Trust, the Beatrice Hankey Foundation, William Temple College, St. Anne's House Soho, the role of the Church in adult education, Religion in the Media, Anglicans and social responsibility, and the Ecumenical Movement. It might also include other aspects of our lives in the world at large, but that is for the future.

The present volume benefits from our annual efforts to tell our relations and friends how the family tried to live amidst the joys and tribulations of those fifty years.

Eberhard George Wedell
September 2012

The Early Years: 1944 – 1964

I went to the London School of Economics in the University of London as an undergraduate in 1944. I was only seventeen, the Higher School Certificate in the war allowing only one year rather than two in the sixth form. During my first year at the LSE it was still evacuated to Cambridge. As soon as the war ended the Air Ministry gave up the LSE buildings in Houghton Street, and we could return. In Cambridge I had an excellent landlady who distinguished herself among other qualities by bringing me a glass of hot milk when I returned from celebrating the end of the war on the 8th of May. In London, accommodation was more difficult. I was fortunate in being offered a back room on the top floor of No 4 Charrington Street in Somerstown. Somerstown was a fairly derelict area between Euston and Saint Pancras stations. So I could cycle down Kingsway to the School. My landlady was Jean Fraser, who was at the time the Youth Secretary of the British Council of Churches. The Council had only been founded in 1942, and it is interesting to reflect on the ecumenical enthusiasm of people like William Temple, who founded it. At that time, the Council included all Christian churches except the Roman Catholics. It is sobering to reflect that the Council was abolished in the 1980s to be replaced by a more inclusive body which the Roman Catholics were willing to join, but which has been much less effective in its actions.

In the middle of the war, when the immediate threat to the country had been averted, the enthusiasm for what might happen after the conflict was substantial. People began to think in terms of reconstruction of the institutions making for peace. For the time being, however, the war had to be pursued. The house in which I had a room belonged to Jim Wilson, grandson of the Antarctic Wilson. He was Warden of the Magdalene College Mission in Somerstown and was a High Anglican. His wife was the daughter of Hubert Peet, the editor of *The Friend* the Quaker journal. Jean Fraser, my immediate landlady was a Presbyterian Deaconess, so the household was ecumenical in composition. My hosts were in fact conscientious objectors to military service and belonged to the Shadwell Group. This was a group of Christian conscientious objectors who were committed to living on the average wage. They were anxious not to be thought to be living at a better level than their contemporaries in the forces.

I came to London, having left Cranbrook, my school, in 1944. My family had moved to Wistow in Leicestershire in 1943, following my mother's appointment to the Directing Staff there, and the start of the training of my sisters for post-war Christian service on the Continent. The creation of the College at Wistow was supported by the British and Foreign Bible Society and was made possible because Lord and Lady Cottesloe had put their house at the College's disposal. The house was a lovely old building set in the rural Leicestershire countryside. It came to have very affectionate memories for Rosemarie and me, since much of our courting took place while she was a student there. I came to Wistow only in the university vacations. In our little community we had much fun and joy together.

My three years at the LSE included a formative experience as President of the Student Christian Movement in the School. The LSE was not noted for its religious convictions. Being the President of a lively Christian society was a challenge, particularly since in 1946 the Churches decided to hold a Mission in the University of London. I suppose it was the last time such an attempt was made. Each of the Colleges of the University was allocated a clerical "missionary". Ours was Ted Wickham, who was at the time the Anglican Industrial Chaplain in Sheffield. Ted and I became lifelong friends. We were later to work together when I was Secretary of the Anglican Board of Social Responsibility. The Mission went well, but there are no records of any conversions. It did however, show that the Church at that time was at least aware of the economic and political circumstances in which the LSE existed.

When I came to the end of my time at the LSE, the Student Christian Movement recruited me as one of its travelling secretaries. I was allocated to the universities in the North of England. These ran from Liverpool in the West via Manchester, Sheffield, and Leeds to Hull in the East, including all the Teacher Training Colleges and other higher education establishments in the area. It was my first acquaintance with industrial Northern England. In the event the family became familiar with it, on and off, since 1947.

At £250 per year, my wages from the SCM made that job a temporary one. After two years I had to begin looking for a career opening. Since I could not be an architect, that being my first choice and too expensive because of a five-year preparation, I decided to apply for the senior branch of the civil service.

The First Division of people working in Whitehall was recruited through a fairly tough selection process conducted by the Civil Service Commission. Honours graduates were admitted to the competition consisting of a written examination and a quite complicated personal selection process. At the time, I was still technically an enemy alien, but that did not prevent me from being considered fairly. In fact, I came out at number four on the list of about twenty successful candidates. I was asked to choose which government department I wanted to join. My first choice was the Colonial Office. In the light of some youthful enthusiastic opinions expressed during the selection process, that was thought to be asking for trouble, so I was allocated to my second choice, the Ministry of Education, and began as an Assistant Principal on the 1st of August 1950. I was paid £450 per year. By that time, I was married to Rosemarie. We wanted to live in Central London so that I could walk to the office in Curzon Street. We were lucky to find the top half of a house in Lower Belgrave Street, on the corner of Eaton Square. This is now one of the most expensive locations in London. At the time the rent was £350 per year, which we could only afford if we let out 2 of our 3 bedrooms. Rosemarie and I were much helped by a loan of £150 from Rachel Heath, who at that time was the Leader of the Blue Pilgrim Fellowship to which we belonged. Florence Cottesloe, the owner of the Wistow, was also one of the Blue Pilgrims. During the latter part of the 1940s Rosemarie and I had been invited to join the Fellowship which was to undertake important work of reconciliation in Germany after war. Rosemarie and I in fact organised a working party of the Fellowship in the Ruhr District of Germany in 1949. Having been trained at Wistow, Rosemarie spent 1947-1948 helping to run the Young Peoples' Programme for her father who was a vicar in a rural part of Westphalia. She then returned to England to marry me, and together we managed the working party in 1949. The Blue Pilgrims had been active in saving people persecuted by the Nazis in Austria in 1938. So they had some idea of the situation into which they were going in Germany. As a result of their working party, a number of young German students joined the Fellowship, which has become an Anglo-German joint operation for many years since then.

Martin, our eldest son, was born in 1950 while we were still living at the home of the Blue Pilgrims, The Chantry in Sevenoaks. We moved to Lower Belgrave Street early in 1951, and from about 1952 we began to invite our friends to coffee parties at our house. That was the beginning of the Chantry Group, whose 60th anniversary we celebrated in 2012.

For the next fourteen years or so, we lived in London. Since we had no capital to buy a house, we moved to ever larger flats as the family grew. When our lease in Lower Belgrave Street expired in 1955, we moved to Prince of Wales Drive facing Battersea Park just south of the river. Crispin, having been born in Belgravia, Philip was born in Battersea and Rebecca was born just after our next move to a five bedroom flat in Queens Club Gardens, West Kensington. At the time these flats were very good value. The five bedroom one we had in Playfair Mansions was set in a garden square with lawns and tennis courts in the middle. The children started at the local primary schools. The intention was that they should later on move on to St Paul's, the independent schools within walking distance. But, of course, my invitation to take the Chair of Adult Education in the University of Manchester changed our plans. In those days, it was not yet the custom for professors to be appointed to universities in one town, and to live possibly a long way away. It was certainly expected that I would move my family to Manchester, so that is where we went, uprooting ourselves from a comfortable way of life in the Metropolis. It was particularly hard for Rosemarie, who had many commitments in London, only some of which could be continued by commuting from Manchester. But little by little, we managed to re-engage there, and of course abroad and in other parts of the world later.

The 1962 letter

THE 1962 LETTER reflects our comfortable and stable life in London; E as the wage earner, and R doing several voluntary jobs. Our life runs in a dual context, with the alternation of town and country made possible by the purchase of Starvecrow, now that the estate on which it stands was being sold. We had already been tenants of the house since 1957. The house stands on the greensand ridge over looking the Weald of Kent. It lies on the far side of Knole Park, east of Sevenoaks. The fast trains from there go to Charing Cross in 35 minutes. We could reach the station in a quarter hour, which made it ideal for E's commuting at weekends and in the holidays. Normally Rosemarie would take the children, the au pair and the two cats by car on Friday afternoons after school. Having settled in at Starvecrow, she would meet my commuter train at Sevenoaks at 7:15.

This moderately idyllic lifestyle was unexpectedly changed by the invitation of the University of Manchester for E to become Professor of Adult Education there.

6 Playfair Mansions
Queen's Club Gardens
London

Christmas 1962

A very happy and blessed Christmas to you from all of us! Encouraged by some of the interesting letters we get at Christmas, which, though duplicated, give us much more news than we should get on a Christmas card, we thought we would return the compliment this year. What with the family, our jobs and other commitments, the time for leisurely letter writing is all but non-existent, so this seems a sensible thing to do.

The year seems to have gone in a flash. Early on we at long last completed the purchase of our tumble-down cottage in Kent which we had occupied for some years on a tied tenancy by virtue of Eberhard's job as a part-time farm labourer. Now that the question of tenure had been settled, "Starvecrow" (an old Kentish name for land which is thought to be so poor that even a crow would starve on it!) is ours. It certainly doesn't look arid and we have a lifetime's work cut out to put the house and the surrounding acre or so of wilderness into shape. This has taken up most of our spare energies at weekends and in the holidays. We have both been surprised at the way in which making things grow has come to satisfy us - neither R nor E ever thought we would make keen gardeners. (We also have a stable near by with water laid on and a meadow in front, which makes a good camping place - in case this should ever be of interest to you).

But life in London has also gone on. R has become much involved in a number of concerns. Among other jobs she is lending a hand with "Christian Family Year" in the Deanery and Diocese and has written one of the discussion pamphlets which the Mothers Union has published. Hers is on "The Christian's private and public responsibility". She has also taken over from a Methodist Minister the writing of a column in the *Fulham Chronicle*, our local weekly. This is quite a chore, but a good counterweight to the household chores, and she seems to have made a friend of the editor. Her group of young wives in the neighbourhood continue to flourish and draw in women who are otherwise pretty much on the margins of the Church.

Eberhard's work as Secretary of the Independent Television Authority has bee fairly demanding on account of the discussion about the future shape of broadcasting which has gone on throughout the year. The job is no bed or roses; not everyone in ITV takes the view that all broadcasting, however financed, must be first and foremost a public service. And the emotionally overcharged atmosphere in which the Pilkington report was written and published has made it more difficult to defend the report against its detractors. But the work is absorbing just because it is in a practical "frontier" situation where ethical theories have constantly to do battle with practical politics.

In March we both flew to the United States, E to look at educational television which has become one of his interests at the Authority, and R to go with him and spend a week with Genia in Boston. We both found the US exhilarating, R being even more enthusiastic than E. What struck us was the extent to which possibilities are still "open" there in a way in which they have long been "closed" in Europe. Anyone can start an enterprise and build up a life for himself without any of the lets and hindrances which are inevitable in the crowded and hide-bound countries on this side of the Atlantic. And the natural manner in which people combine their old ethnic loyalties, whether to Merthyr Tydfil or to Naples., with passionate attachment to the Stars and Stripes is impressive. There are of course other sides to the picture, but by and large we liked what we saw.

EG doesn't have time for much besides the office and the cottage. He did do a stint as an inspector of theological colleges, and was rather shaken by what he inspected. He has now been asked to join the CACTM[1] Inspections Committee. The problems of ordination training and the deployment of clerical manpower are pretty central to whatever can be done structurally about the renewal of the Church, so he is glad to be connected with any attempt to solve them.

The children continue to grow in stature and, we hope, in grace. Martin is now twelve and at Colet Court.[2] He seems to be beginning to get the hang of learning as a deliberate process, if only by dint of very authoritarian cramming. The way in which the traditional method has recently succeeded with him makes us wonder whether the transition from infant school activity methods to more conscious direct teaching is made soon enough in schools today. Crispin (8), Philip (6) and Rebecca (5) are still at the very good new LCC school round the corner. They enjoy life in their various ways; Crispin is learning to swim and to play the recorder; Philip is just getting the knack of reading (and is ploughing through CS Lewis' "The Lion, the Witch and the Wardrobe") and Becca is probably the most musical of the four. She picks out tunes for herself on the piano, and sings at the top of her voice on suitable and unsuitable occasions.

---

[1] CACTM - Central Advisory Council for Training for the Ministry
[2] Colet Court - The Preparatory School for St Paul's School

The 1963 letter is missing

THE 1963 CHRISTMAS letter is missing. So we must assume that the 1962 lifestyle continued until early 1964, when the University of Manchester elected E to his Chair.

The 1964 letter

ROSEMARIE WROTE MOST of the 1964 letter, which reflects our considerable doubts about the move. E had an interesting and in many ways fulfilling job as Secretary of the ITA. He was appreciated by his senior colleagues and the future of the Authority was at that time assured. No one foresaw that the pace of technological and economic change would make the public control system of ITV, which Sir Robert Fraser had built up, redundant within fifteen years. Bernard Sendall, his deputy until his nervous breakdown, and Anthony Pragnell who succeeded him, regarded it as their jobs to "interpret the DG's mind". E's attitude shaped by his perhaps more independent public service approach included positive criticism of some of the DG's policies. The opportunity to develop E's thinking in a more independent context of a University Chair therefore had serious appeal, but for Rosemarie and the children, the move created substantial changes.

18 Cranmer Road,
Didsbury
Manchester 20

11 December 1964

A Christmas letter of any length requires the rare commodities everybody is so short of time and thought. Since I am enjoying a little of both at the moment, I will make a start and send you greetings and our wishes for a blessed Christmas and Happy New Year.

Most of you know by now that we moved to Manchester last September, where E now has the Chair of Adult Education in the University.

I myself resisted the move for quite a while. It is extraordinary how one dreads the loss of a pattern of living one has grown to love. Our comfortable flat in Fulham with its communal gardens and absence of traffic and noise was just tailor-made for us. "Starvecrow" provided the right and regular outlet for us at weekends and during school holidays because of its complete isolation and freedom among fields and woods. In London we were accessible to our friends and at the cottage we could meet as families and exchange children during the holidays.

The children were settled in their schools and three of them could walk there and back. To uproot them seemed so unnecessary. I had had time to develop outside interests such as mental aftercare and rehabilitation with the Richmond Fellowship, contributing to our Fulham local paper, and write the Bible Reading Fellowship Notes. During Christian Family Year I also became very much involved in deanery activities; in our dull and dreary parish, a group of wives and mothers met regularly in each other's houses, and were able to undertake some worthwhile and interesting activities in the parish.

I have told you these things in detail in order to show you what a real adjustment was required of all of us with this move to Manchester. However, it is all over now. In physical terms we are happily and well settled in. The psychological adjustment will take longer, of course.

I won't bore you with the details of our house hunting. We were ignorant about house purchasing and made mistakes. Nevertheless, we are now very much at home in a compact "semi-detached with a difference" (according to an article in Woman's Realm!) in Didsbury, a pleasant and well spoken of inner suburb of Manchester, where many university people live and also send their children to the primary school in Beaver Road.

Or predecessors were a couple well known in Manchester and although they left the house in a state of chaos and desolation so that we had to re-decorate almost all of it, they did some 'open plan' alterations which give the house style. The same applies to the garden. I can cope domestically and was extremely fortunate in finding a successor to my domestic treasure in London. So I am able to continue with my writings and keep up with B.R.F and the Richmond Fellowship. A secretary comes two mornings a week to help with letters and writings.

Manchester, of course, lacks the sophistication of London but is still a homogenous community whose members can get to know each other through common interests and can meet regularly if they want to. In fact one has to guard against becoming drawn into everything.

We had kept in touch through the years with some of the friends we made 17 years ago when we started our married life in Chorlton-on-Medlock. So we were not altogether new and friendless, though the face of Manchester has changed beyond recognition, and Chorlton-on-Medlock has been razed to the ground as part of the redevelopment programme. The new Manchester has yet to emerge; parts that have already done so are promising.

Some of our old friends are now on the staff of the Cathedral. Some new friends are down-town clergy and their wives who meet regularly in order to grapple with the questions and self-criticisms which have been set in motion by *Honest to God, God is No More,* and the books on the new theology.

Those who know them can imagine how lively a time we had recently when Nancy Hoare was staying with us in order to meet Lotte and Werner Pelz who are in Manchester at present. It was just like old Wistow times where we all met in the war.

I am writing this in the train from London to Manchester. Our theological coffee party, now of 14 years' standing, still meets every two months and E and I go up to London while Mrs Chapman and her husband look after the family. I went on to a B.R.F panel meeting. The panel, consisting of Anglican clergy, John Wren-Lewis and myself is concerned to produce bible study outlines for corporate thinking and studying for laity and clergy in parish study groups. We both work on these outlines.

The children settled much more quickly than we expected. The other children in Cranmer Road made our's welcome and accepted them from the beginning Martin, at Manchester Grammar School, feels that there are many similarities between his new school and St Paul's, his old school in London. The new primary school where the others go provides certain problems for Philip and Rebecca coming from a free activity school to one which is bent on producing grammar school material! This has its positive and negative sides. For Rebecca the pressure of work is at present rather much. They all are in the A stream and can cope with it, but Rebecca is the youngest in her form and has a lot to catch up.

Both our parents provide us with food for thought about the problems of old age. E's mother is now widowed and does not find it easy to adjust. My own parents are troubled by the consequences of an operation for cancer which my mother had to have two months ago. Have had a lovely time with them when they were with us last summer, the new of the operation came as a great shock to all of us.

Now for E's job. Besides Adult Education, his department is also concerned with Community Development and has a large contingent of post-graduate students from 14 different countries. He is also Director of the Department of Extra-Mural Studies which provides university extension work for a population of about 4 million people in S.E Lancashire and N.E. Cheshire. The nature and scope of this work is much in flux at present and the university is hoping to strike out on some new lines. The extra mural department has a short-term residential college of its own which provides courses on anything from How to be a Magistrate to the Music of Bartók. E keeps up his links with television by acting as Educational Adviser to one of the television companies - this makes for much fun and much frustration. He is also involved with "New Education", a monthly dealing with new educational methods and techniques, which has just been started.

The 1965 letter

BY CHRISTMAS 1965, most of us had settled well in Manchester. For Rosemarie, in particular, the role of being a professor's wife provided easy access to a career in education. While talking to the City's Chief Education Officer at a university party, the latter offered her a part-time post and she accepted. The post located in Miles Platting, a deprived part of the city. It was effectively the point of entry to Rosemarie's career during the next forty years.

Martin's move from St Paul's (an independent school with class size of about 15) to Manchester Grammar School (a direct grant school with class sizes of nearly 30) was more fraught. Although the High Master of MGS regarded the admission of the children of Professors as a matter of course, Martin and the other boys had to live with rougher and less committed classmates than in London. And that was not easy.

Also, our commuting to Starvecrow in pre-motorway days and the continuing English weather, made that way of life less attractive. I see that even then, we though of looking for "more reliable" weather further south.

18 Cranmer Road,
Didsbury
Manchester 20

14 December 1965

It hardly seems a year since our last letter, and yet so much has happened that it is difficult to know where to start! Since much else hinges on it, we had better report that our original domestic treat lasted only six months. During that time she came to identify herself so much with the family that her husband felt neglected. So we had to put first things first. After a series of failures we started in September with a French au-pair and an excellent help who comes three times a week.

This support on the domestic front made it possible for Rosemarie to start the teaching career she has been thinking about. She now is the religious education specialist in a co-educational secondary modern school in Miles Platting three days a week. As she says:

> the boys and girls are the kind I fell in love with 17 years ago when I ran a mixed youth club in Chorlton-on-Medlock. I am able to share with them my own Christian experience by relating the events of my own life to those of the Bible, which in turn lights up their experience of life. I try not to teach a subject but a way of life, an attitude to people and events, a faith in the goodness of life, the power of love and the promise of change. It is very exciting and I am learning as much, if not more, than they do.

Our own offspring are fit and well. Martin found it more difficult to settle than at first we thought. But he is now beginning to use what Manchester has to offer in the way of music (the Hallé) and the theatre (in particular our new University Theatre which Sybil Thorndike opened in October) etc. In the summer he had a hard but enjoyable three weeks trek with the school in the Western Highlands. Crispin started at Manchester Grammar School in September and thoroughly enjoys it. He runs cross-country, plays chess and the clarinet and sings in the Choral Society. His move leaves Philip as the heard of the family team at Beaver Road, which does him a lot of good. He plays on the recorder ensemble and is developing quite an artistic flair. Becca keeps up her end in her form, although she is the youngest. She now is a Brownie of almost of almost a year's standing and waiting impatiently for her first star.

E's mother was with us for her 75th birthday in March which we celebrated together with Willi and Lisbeth Baermann and Pat Owen, int. al. She also came for various periods in the summer. Both R's parents flew in for three weeks in July, just after E had been put on his back with a slipped disc. As the parents were also invalids to some extent, the household ran as a minor nursing home for a while.

We commuted to Starvecrow for three of the holidays and enjoyed the greater freedom of movement which E's job gives us. But the weather was so poor and the opening and shutting of the house such a bother that we have decided to let it for a while. This will make life less exhausting and give us a chance to go south of the Alps for more reliable weather next summer.

EG's job took him to Paris in January for an educational television committee, to Copenhagen in June for a conference on university adult education and to Salzburg in September for a university summer school. R didn't manage to come on any of these trips, but we did have a long weekend in Berlin together where E was lecturing to the Wistow Reunion. We greatly enjoyed seeing again so many old friends with whom we both spent formative years during the war. The tragedy of Berlin itself hit us hard, as did the extraordinary contrast between the senselessness of the wall and the humanity of the Berliners (presumably on both sides).

Back home we are delighted to see the northward trend continuing: John Davison is joining the Extra-Mural Department in January and there are signs that other friends are moving in the same direction. In the meantime we much enjoy seeing so many of them in one way or another: Nancy Hoare, Bryan Saunders, Carl-Christopher Schweitzer, Vernon Thomas and the Pelz's; John Wren-Lewis and Leslie Paul to do extra-mural lectures; James Mark to lecture on Economic Change in the Adult Education department; and so on. This is just as well since, though E is in London most weeks, R can't get away so easily now. So we have also started to hold weekend meetings of the Theological Coffee Party at The Chantry. A first one last July was a great success and we are meeting there again on January 15-16th.

The 1966 letter

IN 1966, ROSEMARIE'S professional work progressed splendidly. Her commitment to preventing boys and girls "with the one talent" from burying this talent (in the Biblical sense) was strong, and was to become a hallmark of her work in the years to come.

Barbara Pearce's comments on this at Rosemarie's memorial meeting was, I thought, very poignant.

We decided to move Martin to Leighton Park School in Reading because MGS could not really do him justice. The Quaker methods at Reading, whose Headmaster was a friend of Rosemarie's suited him much better and restored his self-confidence at that stage.

The expansion of E's research work in the University was rapid. Adult Education and Social Development marched together in most African countries. So work in Malawi, Zambia, Kenya, and Ethiopia took off. Students from these countries came to Manchester and research into their problems developed on a broad front in 1966-1967, the latter being another year for which there appears to be no Christmas letter.

18 Cranmer Road,
Didsbury
Manchester 20

6 December 1966

Once again our thoughts turn to all our friends to whom this letter brings our warmest wishes for Christmas and the coming year. To start with the children, I am glad to report that Martin did well in his O-levels in June and joined the sixth form at Leighton Park, a progressive Quaker school at Reading which offers what is best in the Quaker spirit and tradition, in September. He has settled down quickly and happily. History is his forte and he will concentrate on this for his A-levels, together with French and Geography.

Crispin is developing a strong bent for analysis, a flair for languages and real musicality. He plays the clarinet in the school's windband, is captain of his form's rugger-team, and a good swimmer and long-distance runner.

Philip has come on surprisingly, and currently combines a highly developed imagination with an acute sense of observation. He loves writing imaginary tales and devours books (he has just emerged from *Lord of the Flies*). He is also greatly attached to his hamster, Henry, plays centre-half in the school team and is a good swimmer. He will take the MGS entrance exam in February.

Rebecca will probably become the mathematician in the family. So far she is a good all-rounder with a bent for practical problems. But she also enjoys reading. She, Phil and I go swimming on Saturday mornings, and after initial fears and hesitations she is coming on well. She also enjoys making music and is in the school choir and recorder ensemble, as well as in the mathematical club.

My mother died last Ascension day. She was fully conscious of the meaning of that day for her and we are thankful that it happened very quickly. Although we were so far apart we were always in each other's hearts, and I have lost my best friend in her. My father has accepted her loss with great fortitude, for which my sisters and I are very thankful. We are expecting E's mother on December 14th, for a month or two.

The whole family enjoyed a glorious month in the sun at La Escala on the Costa Brava. If I were to put down all our experiences, it would fill pages. We rented a flat and Vernon Thomas joined us for a fortnight during which we did most of our excursions and had lively discussions about Harvey Cox's admirable book *The Secular City*. We hope to go again sometime. On the way out through France by car we found ourselves one night quite by chance in the village inn at Nohan, opposite the manor house where Georges Sand used to live. The next day being Sunday, the cheap day for Museums in France, we walked round the delightful and civilised domain where she and Chopin worked and entertained a galaxy of European intellectuals and artists. On the return journey we spent a night at Chartres. The windows of the cathedral far exceed expectation, though the children were too occupied with counting the steps up the tower to take them in.

I teach every morning now, and the second year is easier for obvious reasons. I have worked out my own syllabus, relating current events to the lives and times of the men and women of the Bible and vice versa. To try to think and act biblically is a fascinating exercise, emotionally and intellectually satisfying, and cuts the ice with my pupils. I think the realities of the Kingdom have always come alive when men and women were able to think and act in this way, i.e. were aware that adventure exploration, change and flexibility, are of the essence of the biblical faith. It is impossible to separate the Old and New Testaments, or to speak of one having superseded the other. The more I study the Old the more I find the New in it. Jesus knew he was the product of the law and the prophets, and applied their teaching to a new and challenging situation, as we all must do. The semi-literate boys and girls I teach are very largely those with the one talent, and it is my job to prevent them from burying it. All this goes on in the context of our social history, which is a part of the unfolding pattern of the Kingdom.

Our tenant at Starvecrow turned out to be a bad lot. He is now behind bars (not on our account!) and we are trying to repair the ravages of his occupation. On the credit side, four years of struggle with the Electricity Board have brought their price for connecting us down to manageable limits, so that we are now on the mains, a luxury we though we should never achieve.

EG's work is pretty absorbing but very satisfying. The research section which he started now has five members, the number of postgraduate students is up to about 50, about half from the UK, the rest from all over the world. In January he is spending three weeks in East and Central Africa to look at social development. His book on broadcasting and public policy is making slow progress: it will be touch and go to finish it by the end of March.

The 1967 letter is missing

THE LOSS OF the 1967 letter means that there is a lot that happened in 1966-68 which is not chronicled here.

The Holly Royde extensions were, in fact, quite a revolution in the University's approach to its post-experience education. I regarded the primitive conditions going back to the war years where five course members shared a bedroom, as quite unacceptable for the modern age. I therefore insisted on providing civilised living and learning conditions at our short-term residential college, and set about creating these. An appeal by the university's Chancellor, the Duke of Devonshire, raised only about £30,000, but the University invested another £60,000 in order to do the job properly. At the end of 1968 we invited Mr R A Butler, the Minister of Education in Mr Churchill's wartime cabinet and the author of the 1944 Education Act, to open the extensions. Holly Royde became a modern residential college where responsible adults could be expected to stay. The University Grants Committee still refused to pay for private baths and lavatories, so these had to be shared, but the ingenious design of the octagon opening out into the garden became, at the time, the most agreeable facility for Adult Education in the country. The comfortable environment, together with the intellectual level of the learning opportunities provided, made the University's Adult Education attractive to important policy-influencing activities. We launched the Holly Royde Symposia on Broadcasting Policy, meetings on Consumer Protection and the Control of Advertising, all of them areas in which development was needed.

The 1968 Letter

HAVING MICHAEL ELLIOTT and his colleagues at the University Theatre from 1968 changed the University's attitude to its drama policy. The University had been building a well equipped theatre for its drama courses. Our professor of Drama, Hugh Hunt, had been Director of the Old Vic Theatre in London. Michael Elliott was a family friend of mine. So when he came to Manchester to ask whether we could make arrangements to receive their company, Hugh Hunt and I encouraged them to come. Michael brought a distinguished group of actors and directors who had found London's West End theatrical standards unattractive. After a period at the Hammersmith Theatre in the late 1950s, they hoped to find a more steady audience in Manchester.

At the same time efforts were made to create in Manchester a second home for the top quality opera productions from Covent Garden. A local entrepreneur had spent about five million pounds to adapt the Palace Theatre for their productions. But unfortunately the complications of securing top quality singers for Manchester periods failed. Nor were the city fathers willing to spend money on supporting an opera company of our own and Opera North went to Leeds. So in 2012 we have one of the best opera houses in the country at the Lowry Centre in Salford, but only the inside of two weeks of opera a year which are provided by Opera North from Leeds.

18 Cranmer Road,
Didsbury
Manchester 20

December 1968

Greetings to you once again for Christmas and New Year. As I read through the letters we sent you in past years I realise how much the rate of change in the world at large is affecting us all in our thinking and living. At the same

16

time the daily round seems excessively normal and it fills most of the horizon, particularly for the children.

Martin left Leighton Park in the summer, and has been having some History tutoring here in the University during the Autumn. On the strength of some good A level results he has been offered a place at Canterbury and has also been taking the college entrance exam at Cambridge. We enjoy having him at home again, and he too sees the pro's and as well as the con's of family life more than before. At present he is doing night work at the Post Office's international sorting office in town. After Christmas he hopes to get a full time job until early summer in order to earn the necessary money to buy his dream car. He has taken up the piano again and goes on developing his style in art and design.

Crispin likes to sit at his desk and get on with his work. He produces good essays and poems. His flair for language is developing and he thinks he will continue with Russian, which he is now doing for the second year, in the Sixth Form next autumn. Both he and Philip have made interesting contacts with French families and benefit from their annual exchanges. Crispin's clarinet playing is improving steadily and he won a music prize in the summer. He also plays piano duets with Becca. His enthusiasm for sport has waned a bit and he needs to be prodded to exert himself in that direction With a certain amount of humming and having he continues to visit Mrs Brown as part of the School's youth community service project.

Philip "throws himself with enthusiasm into everything he does" according to his last MGS report, and s seems to have settled down as happily and successfully as Crispin in that large and interesting school. Rugger is his main preoccupation. He plays inside centre for the Under Fourteens. But he also sings in the Choir which is busy rehearsing the Messiah with the Orchestra for next Monday. Apart from that he swims and debates regularly, draws and still devours books.

Becca moved to Withington High School in September. She is settling down and making new friends. Games are also her main interest - she plays netball with gusto and has been doing quite a lot of riding at weekends. At Whitsun she and Cathryn Lanyon did some energetic pony trekking in Wales. Her music is coming on well under an excellent piano teacher; she has just done her grade 3 exam. I am beginning to appreciate her help in the kitchen at weekends; in fact all four support us valiantly in house and garden.

Building projects have taken up a good deal of our time. Most of the year weekend visitors had to suffer a tour of E's particular baby, the extensions at Holly Royde College. Mercifully these are now completed and were opened by Rab Butler at the end of October. At home we took the garden side off the house and put it back again so as to enlarge the drawing room and give the dining room a view. While we were at it we also abandoned our ruinous electric heating for gas. It seemed as though the work would never end; but it has. Now all that remains is E's fussing with a complicated set of thermostats and time clocks.

His broadcasting book came out in April and was well received in the press; the broadcasters themselves found it too hot to handle. But the book's thesis is beginning to assert itself, if only by the logic of events. E went to Malawi again in September to help the University to set up its Centre for Continuing Education. He also visited Zambia and Ethiopia where Manchester alumni now direct both the Social Welfare and the Community Development Departments.

We enjoy having Michael Elliott and the 69 Theatre Company at the University Theatre. Their production of Ibsen's *When We Dead Awaken* with Wendy Hiller was a remarkable achievement: the play must be one of the most unactable ever written! With this standard at the University, a new National Film Theatre, the local cultural scene has begun to be a good deal brighter.

I am teaching at a new school in a different part of Manchester. We are multi-racial and multi-religious and have 70% immigrant children. This is a stimulating and challenging situation taxing one's imaginative resources to the utmost. I do Comparative Religion as part of a project involving the Geography, Science, and Art teachers as well as myself under a new integrated curriculum development scheme with one of the 5th year groups. Our theme is "the human family and its home". We aim to help our young people to become aware that each of the subjects is part of the whole body of human knowledge, that the whole world is our home and that true believers of all faiths are united in their passion for truth and goodness. I am glad to be involved in this way in the great opportunities we have in this country of making the fact come alive in our schools, families, neighbourhoods and cities that mankind is one.

May the inspiration of the Prince of Peace speed the work of His kingdom everywhere in 1969.

The 1969 letter

L OOKING BACK FROM 2012, the change in East-West relations in 1969 remains remarkable. At the time, we thought the "Cold War" was a permanent condition of our life. As reported in 1969 Rosemarie had in Berlin, and EG in Austria, occasional glimpses of life in Eastern Europe. We did not realise at the time that the evolution of education and of technology would make people unwilling to accept the inhuman character of Soviet style policy. In fact of course the whole system of the Cold War would be overturned by popular revolt twenty years later.

EG's British Council visit to Israel was instigated by their reaction to his book on *Broadcasting and Public Policy*. It was thought by Israel's new television authority to be relevant to the development of their system. Elihu Katz, an American at the Hebrew University, had been asked by the government to act as Director General of the new Israel Broadcasting Corporation. His approach to public service broadcasting was similar to mine as outlined in the book. Following a successful series of lectures, Katz continued to keep in contact and eventually became a Simon Fellow in Manchester for the academic year 1972-73. During that year we were, as recounted later, to develop our joint Ford Foundation Project on Broadcasting in the Third World which made for much work during 1973-75.

18 Cranmer Road,
Didsbury
Manchester 20

December 1969

As we settle down to write our Christmas letter we find that most of our doings during the year have bee fairly routine. Everyone has been occupied in unspectacular ways: Rosemarie more deeply involved in work with a variety of groups; Martin driving a fork-lift truck at Kellogg's Cornflakes factory before going up to Eliot College at Canterbury in October; Crispin mainly busy with this clarinets and music; Philip struggling against odds to keep his rugger team together; Becca living her life as it comes and E seemingly busy with the care and maintenance of his University departments.

But, more closely observed, a lot of seemingly humdrum works has made for interesting encounters and experiences. Rosemarie is working with an all West Indian Group for the Certificate of Secondary Education in Religious Knowledge. Under the umbrella theme of 'Caring for Others' she is taking them through the Old and New Testaments and tracing the growth of the mustard seed into the complex tree of the modern industrial welfare system. Workers in statutory and voluntary welfare agencies contribute to the course. The house group which originated from R's membership of the Executive Committee of the Council of Christians and Jews decided to broaden its scope in the autumn and to include members of other faiths living in the city.

These activities led to R's being appointed to a commission set up by the British Council of Churches to work out a statement on the theology of race. The commission includes both parsons and lay people, workers with immigrants and social scientists. It represents all shades of churchmanship and a wide range of opinions.

The summer we spent with our grandparents and at conferences. Having all driven together to Dusseldorf, R and Crispin went to an Anglo-Dutch-German meeting of the Blue Pilgrims in Berlin. They saw a good deal of the situation in the East of the city and, as R reports, "returned with the strong impression that the Christians in East Germany have reached an important turning point in their relationship with their Marxist compatriots. After treating the communist government for twenty years as a transitory political structure, they are now beginning to accept that it has come to stay and that they have a responsibility to seek a creative dialogue with it. The example of their brethren in Poland and Czechoslovakia, who have been doing this for many years, is now beginning to be seen as relevant".

In the meantime E with Philip and Becca went to Salzburg for the conversations on adult education which the Austrians organise each year and which provide the most effective point of contact between adult educators in East and West. The role of adult education within the sociopolitical structure of a country is, as it turned out, a fairly reliable indicator of its social philosophy! On the way back they spent some time at Seibersbach in order to help E's mother to sell her house prior to her move to more manageable quarters at Düsseldorf. Then we all met at Volmerdingsen to celebrate R's father's eightieth birthday. En route E and Martin learned the value of seat belts as the car skidded and overturned in a cloudburst. The car was a write-off.

Martin had two cars during the year, one bought for £10 and another for £35. The latter survived long enough to take him and his chattels to Canterbury where he is reading Social Sciences. Life by all accounts is cheerful, though the winds on the downs above the city come straight from the North Pole.

Crispin, now in the Lower Sixth, decided to do English, Russian and French. He finds literary criticism hard going and is cutting his philosophical teeth on a very able set of masters. His social and musical round is pretty dizzy. He has just succeeded in getting into the Lancashire Youth orchestra, which rehearses all over the County, so that it looks as though he will become even more peripatetic.

Two members of Philip's team in the rugger club broke a leg during the term; he himself was out of action for a while with an injured thumb. All this and the haphazard training arrangements at the school conspired to give them a bad season. But they battle on undaunted by defeats. In spite of the surfeit of music provided by Crispin and Becca, Phil has let himself be persuaded to try an instrument. He chose the guitar and now strums in strictest privacy under the guidance of a charming West Indian student from Sheffield who is studying at the Royal College.

Becca is another games fiend. She plays whatever is going: hockey, lacrosse, netball, not to mention the French horn. This enables her to join in the orchestra. Work does not loom large and she just about gets by. She and Martin have developed an enthusiasm for stamp collecting for which there is little hereditary justification.

EG has been at home for most of the year. In April he did a British Council lecture tour in Israel and so had his first visit to Holy Land. It was a great advantage no to be a 'pilgrim' but to be doing an ordinary job, thus the level of expectation was not artificially inflated and he was able to experience the country and its people at their different levels; biblical, political and human. To be eating St Peter's fish in a kibbutz on the Sea of Galilee in the lee of the Golan Heights provided the conflation of all three levels which is the reality of Israel today. His most memorable visit was to the educational complex at Sde Boker in the Negev desert. The arid zone studies carried on in that wilderness aims to harness an all but impossible environment to the service of man as much by teaching people how to live in the desert as by making the desert bloom.

A lecture EG had to give at Teilifís Éireann justified a brief trip together to

Ireland in February. We had hoped to motor to the West cost, but the weather was so icy that we had to stay in Dublin, snugly ensconced in the Shelbourne. So we had a night at the Gate Theatre with "Patrick O'Shaughnessy goes to Maynooth" and another at the Royal with "Big Maggie." Nowhere have we seen participant theatre in the same way: the audience was as good as the actors. We fell for the city and its people.

The 1970 letter

IN THE MEANTIME, EG had been asked by UNESCO to undertake a study in Cyprus for a possible higher education institution in that island. Because of the pressure of his full-time work in Manchester in term time, he said that he could only go to Cyprus in the vacation. The result was a series of four visits, lasting four weeks at a time, during which he developed is recommendations and left his Cypriot colleagues to work on them in his absence. The report helped the Cyprus government to develop its ideas about higher education. In the event, they went further than the training of teachers and in due course, launched a university of their own. The continuing inability of the Greeks and the Turks thirty years later to find a formula appropriate to their membership of the European Union leave the Cyprus higher education system handicapped to this day.

In July 1970, EG directed the first of the series of annual seminars on Social and Physical Planning for American town planners. It appeared early in the year that Manchester's planning procedures were appreciated in the United States. The University's Planning Department and its architects and social policy staff were willing to provide a three-week course on their methods. I directed the course in the context of Continuing Education for these professional workers from America. It continued for three or four years.

18 Cranmer Road,
Didsbury

Second Sunday in Advent 1970

It is time to get down to our Christmas greeting to you: the more so as we hope to do some skiing over Christmas. We are going to Sauze d'Oulx in the Piedmont Alps this time. Since our last expedition three years ago only Philip has been keeping his skiing up, so the rest of us need to limber up intensively between now and then.

We are all ready for a change or a rest since the term, and indeed the year, has been pretty busy. Now that R has begun to work towards an M.A. thesis in Comparative Religion with Professor Brandon here in the University she has been as tied to her books in the evenings as Martin who has just taken his preliminary exams at Canterbury; Crispin who is taking A levels next summer; and Philip doing the same for O levels. Only Becca and EG aren't working for exams. But he is currently commuting to Cyprus under UNESCO auspices in order to help the Cyprus Government to establish as Institute of Higher Education, and this tends to concentrate his work at home into 2/3 the normal span of weeks at a time. He is off again for fie weeks after Christmas and a further stint at Easter, by which time the project should be under way.

That leaves Becca who has shot up in the last few months and is now a regular flapper. Games are still her main preoccupation and life at school and at home is cheerful and uncomplicated. In an attempt to instil some edge to her piano playing R has recently put her to work with Iso Elinson's widow who is a teacher of substance (in every way). Having got used to her rather formidable manner, Becca is beginning to see the difference between performance and interpretation. R has also at Mrs Elinson's instigation taken up her singing again and has discovered that there's nothing wrong with her voice and that she enjoys singing Silcher and Schubert Lieder as much as ever. They are now thinking of doing a serenade concert together in the Octagon at Holly Royde.

R is also more deeply involved in the educational work of the Manchester Council for Community Relations. The Inter-Faith group she runs seems to be the only context in which serious conversation about matters of ultimate concern goes on between the Christian, Jewish, Muslim and Buddhist comities in these parts. Whenever there is a gap in expertise one or other of EG's overseas students can usually be found with the required background. But on the whole the size and substance of the various ethnic groups in the city has thrown up leaders able to work amicably and constructively together, so that there is no material here to support Powellite arguments of any sort. But then Manchester has been absorbing, and benefiting from, immigrants ever since it began to grow in the early 19th century, so there is a good tradition on which to build.

Martin hopes to hear before Christmas whether his concentration to work this last term has made up for his leisurely first year. Stop press: All is well. He has found his reading in Law beginning to engage him (shades of his grandfather?) but on the whole he thinks he will concentrate on Economic History for his Part II. In August and September he toured Italy in a jeep an HMI, whom we last knew at Wistow in 1946; and so on. The flow of academic visitors from all parts of the world grows apace, so that we have had to allocate one of the staff to look after them all. Elihu Katz, director of the Communications Institute at the University of Jerusalem, is with us as a Simon fellow and has succeeded Bryan Saunders as a Broomcroft resident. Elihu and EG are about to begin a joint research project on Broadcasting and National Development in the developing countries. This will run until the summer of 1975 and will involve a series of case studies of countries in Asia, Africa, Latin America and the Pacific. The project is funded by the Ford Foundation through the International Broadcast Institute.

With all the visitors and new commitments R is as busy as ever. She is chairman of a new play centre in Longsight, one of the deprived areas of the city. The need for this emerged from a discussion with Mrs Scott, one of our helpers. It is run by local parents, university students and voluntary helpers and is an interesting example of Community Action. Her Inter-faith Group has become an established part of the Manchester community relations scene. It is sprouting new ventures such as a day-long Inter-faith Dialogue at Holly Royde College as part of the Manchester Festival next May. Although all these activities touch directly only a tiny proportion of the population, local and immigrant, they seem to contribute to the unusually positive community relations in the city by enabling some of the leading members of the various communities to meet at the personal level and to discover each other as human beings and fellow citizens.

We await news from Martin about whether he managed to get to Cape Kennedy in time for the blast-off of Apollo 17 last week. M completed his Economic and Social History course at Canterbury in the summer with quite a good 2.1, on the strength of which he was immediately offered a research studentship. But he had arranged to spend some months in North America with two friends. They flew to Ontario in July to pick tobacco on the shores of Lake Erie in order to earn enough money for a Greyhound bus ticket round the periphery of the United States. His plans now include a visit to the Caribbean and we don't expect to see him back much before Easter unless he is offered a 'stage' with the European Communities Commission in Brussels which begins in February.

The University also is beginning to gird its loins for entry to the Common Market and has just launched the country's first higher degree in European Community Studies. EG's Department is contributing an option in European Community Policies in the belief that success or failure will in the last resort depend on whether the peoples of Europe see themselves as sharing a

1. Early Spring in Manchester: March 1965
Rosemarie, Gertrude, Rebecca, EGW, Crispin and Philip.

2. Rosemarie and Martin with a Chinese friend in the garden in Didsbury 1990s.

5. A family Brunch at Cranmer Road, 1995.

6. An alfresco Luncheon Party of the European Institute for the Media at Cranmer Road.

with some friends of his who are studying architecture, having spent a bucolic July picking fruit in Herefordshire. So he did not come with us to Calpe; nor did Crispin who was invited to join the civic youth part on this year's exchange visit to Leningrad. The Manchester-Leningrad link goes back to the dark days of the war and has survived all ups and downs since then. There was some discussion about breaking it off after both Hungary and during the Czech invasion, but it has always been argued that these contacts should be kept. And there must now be a substantial body of young Mancunians and Leningraders whose attitudes have been significantly affected by these carefully prepared and executed visits in both directions. Crispin for one found it a great experience, largely at the human level. The Hermitage, opera and ballet and the last two days in Moscow all added to the impact. He thinks that the young in Russia have tremendous advantages but that these are largely unmatched by the opportunities open to adults. Once in a job life seems to him to close in on people, with far few opportunities for continued development than in the West. Philip's somewhat reluctant exercursus into music which we reported last year has turned into a real affection for his guitar. He now plays quite expertly and still works with Evan Crawford. His enthusiasm for rugger has waned a bit, though he continues to play and unlike his brother is as keen on fitness as ever.

The parents, Philip and Becca spent August in Calpe. The flat of which we have a share has a magnificent view of the sea and the Penon de Ifach, the local Rock of Gibraltar. Although the spoliation of this part of the Spanish coast has progressed a good deal since we first went there two years ago Calpe remains one of the pleasanter places partly because the main coast road runs behind rather than through it and also because the old town retains its charm and integrity at the top of the hill where it was built for fear of Algerian pirates, leaving the rash of skyscrapers to fight it out below on the way to the beach. W are fortunate in being all but at the bottom with only one vacant ex-vineyard between us and the beach. So far discord in the owner's family has prevented them from building on it and blocking our view. Long may it remain so. We greatly enjoyed the sun and water with plenty of snorkelling among the reefs just off the beach. We also explored the hinterland including Elche, a fascinating town a little way inland from Alicante, which boasts both the earliest mystery play in Europe and its largest palm forest. We just missed the former during which angels are energetically hoisted up and down the dome of the cathedral on ropes. Not one of the least achievements of the holidays was that R finally capitulated and learned to make a fourth at bridge. By the end she had developed into quite a formidable partner.

with some friends of his who are studying architecture, having spent a bucolic July picking fruit in Herefordshire. So he did not come with us to Calpe; nor did Crispin who was invited to join the civic youth part on this year's exchange visit to Leningrad. The Manchester-Leningrad link goes back to the dark days of the war and has survived all ups and downs since then. There was some discussion about breaking it off after both Hungary and during the Czech invasion, but it has always been argued that these contacts should be kept. And there must now be a substantial body of young Mancunians and Leningraders whose attitudes have been significantly affected by these carefully prepared and executed visits in both directions. Crispin for one found it a great experience, largely at the human level. The Hermitage, opera and ballet and the last two days in Moscow all added to the impact. He thinks that the young in Russia have tremendous advantages but that these are largely unmatched by the opportunities open to adults. Once in a job life seems to him to close in on people, with far few opportunities for continued development than in the West. Philip's somewhat reluctant exercursus into music which we reported last year has turned into a real affection for his guitar. He now plays quite expertly and still works with Evan Crawford. His enthusiasm for rugger has waned a bit, though he continues to play and unlike his brother is as keen on fitness as ever.

The parents, Philip and Becca spent August in Calpe. The flat of which we have a share has a magnificent view of the sea and the Penon de Ifach, the local Rock of Gibraltar. Although the spoliation of this part of the Spanish coast has progressed a good deal since we first went there two years ago Calpe remains one of the pleasanter places partly because the main coast road runs behind rather than through it and also because the old town retains its charm and integrity at the top of the hill where it was built for fear of Algerian pirates, leaving the rash of skyscrapers to fight it out below on the way to the beach. W are fortunate in being all but at the bottom with only one vacant ex-vineyard between us and the beach. So far discord in the owner's family has prevented them from building on it and blocking our view. Long may it remain so. We greatly enjoyed the sun and water with plenty of snorkelling among the reefs just off the beach. We also explored the hinterland including Elche, a fascinating town a little way inland from Alicante, which boasts both the earliest mystery play in Europe and its largest palm forest. We just missed the former during which angels are energetically hoisted up and down the dome of the cathedral on ropes. Not one of the least achievements of the holidays was that R finally capitulated and learned to make a fourth at bridge. By the end she had developed into quite a formidable partner.

All July EG directed what is likely to be the first of a series of annual seminars on Social and Physical Planning for American town planners and social interventionists of various kinds. It appeared earlier in the year that Manchester was regarded by the Americans as the ideal place to study the way in which this country copes with its urban problems. So we had an instructive and lively time with about 45 Americans. Although we have, for various reasons, managed to develop a more coherent approach to planning over here, we found the Americans to be much more thoughtful and articulate about the social objectives of physical planning. The Adult Education Department is fuller than ever and makes a lot of work. Both the idea of community work and the concept of continuing education are beginning to become politically important, and growing numbers of people want to find out what substance there is in them. The University at large survived two sit-ins and is learning quite a lot from all this unrest. It will be a little time, though, before the right mix of participation merges. At present we are merely piling Pelion on Ossa in the way of consultative committees of all kinds, which for some of us reduce the working day to little more than a long string of meetings.

Just as this letter was about to be set up, new of Opi's death was phoned through. It was not unexpected but hurt nevertheless because at such times distances assert their cruel reality. R will be flying out for the funeral on Saturday. It is fitting that her father should have departed during Advent, a time he filled so richly for his daughters with the expectant joyfulness of the German Advent season. He was a poet and a singer as well as churchman of the Lutheran church, and on St Nicolas' day, December 6th particularly, he would visit his large office where his family and office staff, assembled together, were expecting him. In the disguise of St. Nicholas he would prepare them for the coming of the Christchild with a special poem for everyone present, conduct the Advent singing and bestow a bagful of nuts and Advent biscuits on each. Especially during the dark days of National Socialism these events shone as a warm and comforting light. To him we owe political awareness and commitment and our mourning is mingled with joy and gratitude.

The 1971 letter

THE CYPRUS PROJECT was completed at Easter 1971. Having just cleared up that assignment, EG was asked by the World Bank to assemble and lead a team to advise them on how to spend seven million dollars on educational development in Malawi. There was ample competence on education, economics, and agriculture development in the University, so it was not difficult to assemble a team of six people who spent three weeks in Malawi. In order to get round the country fairly quickly, we rented an aeroplane which just took our team members. Malawian airstrips in those days had no lighting, so we had to take off and land in daylight. What struck us forcibly was that the village schools that existed need to be available to the whole population, not only to children of school age. So we suggested that schools should operate all day, not only in school hours, and that the staff should be able to help the adults in the village to cope with their development problems. Unfortunately the then president of Malawi, Mr Banda, had had his education in Scotland and thought Scottish grammar schools were the answer to his problems. So he resisted our advice, and the World Bank had to spend their money on a much more restricted range of educational opportunities than we recommended.

At home, Crispin's clarinet playing was so good that he was invited to join the National Youth Orchestra of the United Kingdom. At the same time, Philip started preparing for his A levels, and became the only member of the family to opt for Mathematics with Statistics as one of his three A level subjects.

18 Cranmer Road,
Didsbury
Manchester 20

Third Sunday in Advent 1971

I see we are a week later than last year with this letter! Mercifully there are almost four whole weeks of Advent, so that it may yet reach you in time. Now that the last days for the Christmas post are announced on the radio every morning, we are constantly reminded of our lack of system in this as in other matters.

We shall be at home this Christmas: all in all everyone prefers this to the erratic Christmas habits we have encountered on our skiing expeditions. Last year, though, we did enjoy the skiing at Sauze d'Oulx tremendously. It was one of the few places to have had a good snowfall early in the seasons, so that we lost no time as at Obladis. A further six inches or so on Boxing Day gave pretty well perfect conditions for the rest of our stay. The children passed their Ski Club tests and were rewarded with a bronze medal. R practised her skating and in spite of a nasty fall was pleased with her achievement. It revived many happy childhood memories. EG had a lot of fun reviving his antiquated pre-war style. Martine complemented skill with verve. Seeing him charging down the steepest piste regardless, with mane and beard flying, one of the instructors was heard to shout 'Look out, here comes Jesus'.

At Easter EG finished his consultancy in Cyprus where R joined him for a fortnight. Since it was the wettest April in living memory, the reputed beauty of the Island in the spring remains to be tested. But we were much spoilt by our Cypriot friends. The report on the proposed Institute of Education was published by UNESCO in July and seems to have a reasonable chance of being implemented. EG found it a useful exercise in participative planning; his Cypriot colleagues contributed a great deal to the project and can thus see the outcome as in a real sense their own, rather than something imported by one of the itinerant 'experts' whom developing countries suffer so patiently. Having barely cleared up that assignment, EG was asked by the World Bank to collect and lead a team from the University in a study of the education sector in Malawi. This more complicated exercise is till going on.

R is well dug in to her work on Comparative Religion. Having been made a JP early in the year, she found the two commitments too much in practice and so has resigned from the Commission of the Peace. Now with reasonable domestic support she can spend part of every day at the University. The sudden death of Samuel Brandon, her professor and supervisor, has been a great blow. He was a good friend and a scholar well ahead of his time. R now feels at home in the religious milieu of Buddhism and Hinduism, and is fascinated by her discoveries of the economic, cultural and religious cross-fertilisation which has been going on between Asia and the West since the first "urban revolution" far back in BC2000, greatly assisted by the empire-building of Cyrus the Great and Alexander the Great. She recommends for your reading Trevor Ling's *A History of Religion East and West* in paperback.

Martin is in his final year at Canterbury and appears to be developing into a passable economic historian. He thinks that the academic life is one of the few tolerable means left of earning a livelihood in the modern world, and seems inclined to try it. If he does well enough he may go abroad for some advanced work next autumn. Much of his time has been spent earning the money needed to buy and run a car. The ups and downs of this endeavour are too complicated for a Christmas letter: but after various false starts he seems now to have found a vehicle that runs.

Crispin's year has been dominated by music, with the occasional interruption for English, French and Russian, his A level subjects. What with the National Youth Orchestra, the Lancashire Youth Orchestra and various local ensembles, he has been fully stretched and we have argued the pro's and con's of making a career in music. Alongside his preparation for university entrance he is doing a GCE music course for interest. He is thinking of leaving school at Easter to take a job before joining a socio-geographical expedition to Iran which a group of masters is mounting. As a non-geographer he was rather pleased to be selected.

Philip continued as the family fitness fiend. He cycles to school, exercises with his bullworker (a fearsome device designed to develop every conceivable muscle) and has returned to the Rugger Club as a regular wing three-quarter for the second fifteen. Having done the agreed year of guitar lessons he thinks he has had enough, which is a pity. But like Martin he seems to have a flair for drawing and design. He and a friend now do a regular commitment in the geriatric ward at Withington Hospital. His O levels were creditable and he is (so far) the only member of the family to be capable of doing Maths-with-Statistics in the sixth form. He combines this with French and History.

Life for Becca goes on its accustomed way. Hockey, netball and lacrosse takes up a lot of her time at weekends, and her musical activities at school and with Mrs Elinson give her a lot of stimulus. She is also now taking German and is beginning to get some system into her home-grown version of the language. Recently she suffered EG's performance at the school founders' day: it is still not clear who was more apprehensive, Becca about what bricks her father would drop or EG at the prospect of addressing 600 girls! But all was well.

In the larger context of the University the move of William Temple Foundation from the relative isolation of Rugby onto the University campus was completed during the year. Relieved of the financial and operational problems of maintaining residential plant, the staff can devote the resources of the Foundation to research and development in the field where money is otherwise so hard to find. They also have the stimulus of a large academic community (in particular the link with Ronald Preston's new Department of Social and Pastoral Theology).

R's paring down of her non-academic activities has not included the inter-faith group. From this developed a very good weekend organised by a young rabbi, Jeffrey Newmon, with Christian, Muslim, Jewish and Buddhist speakers and a late night session on the Kabbala. The latest addition to the group is the new Imam of Manchester. She also continues with her membership of the MCCR's education committee which is proving quite an effective pressure group for the bringing about of a greater awareness of our emerging multi-religious and multi-cultural society.

There is now also hope that Michael Elliott's 69 Theatre Company will get its permanent Manchester base. We would like to see it as the nucleus of a National Theatre of the North. Whether the Arts Council, the City and community at large will pull together well enough to achieve this, remains to be seen.

The 1972 letter

EG HAD FOR some years been one of the governors of William Temple College in Rugby. The College had been founded as a national memorial to Archbishop William Temple, a particularly distinguished Archbishop during the Second World War. It was felt that his far-reaching ideas about the Church's impact on Society required a place where other people could learn about them, and the Church as a whole could implement them. Unfortunately the money collected for this purpose was inadequate and the College was in constant financial difficulty because its residential accommodation could not make a profit. I suggested to the governors that if they could move to our university, they could use the university's residential accommodation without too much capital commitment. For that reason, the governors decided to accept the invitation of the Manchester Business School to use accommodation there and to provide residential places in university residences and at Holly Royde College. In addition to the move to Manchester, William Temple College had to find a suitable Director. Canon David Jenkins, who was at the time working with the World Council of Churches, was appointed. After two or three years, he transferred to Leeds University as Professor of Theology, and two or three years later, was appointed Bishop of Durham. The College has carried on for these decades without fulfilling the promise with which it was created.

Having appointed Michael Elliott to direct the University Theatre, we needed to find a larger auditorium for his productions. The University Theatre with four hundred seats was essentially a demonstration space, not a commercial proposition. Robert Scott, Michael's Manager, looked out for a bigger space. This he found in the Royal Exchange in the centre of the city. This splendid building had been created to accommodate the Cotton Trade. The demise of cotton meant that the exchange was, by 1972, empty. Robert Scott persuaded the City Council to make it available to the Theatre and the directors, of whom I was one, decided to go for a Theatre in the Round. That theatre has now been operating for almost forty years and has become exceptionally successful in attracting a steady local audience.

By 1972, the UK's membership of the European Economic Community was promoted by the government. The University decided to launch a post-graduate course to prepare experts to take part in the Community. This ran for a number of years and was quite important for those of us who believed that the UK's future was closely linked to this European initiative. EG found himself solicited to work at the European Commission's Headquarters in Brussels because of his experience of vocational training for adults needing to change their professional profiles. The University was willing to give him two year's leave of absence, and he started commuting to Brussels by air in the autumn of 1973. Since Rebecca was in her last year of school, we decided that Rosemarie would stay in Manchester until Rebecca finished her schooling. EG commuted from Sunday night to Friday between Manchester and Brussels until 1976.

18 Cranmer Road,
Didsbury
Manchester 20

Second Sunday in Advent 1972

The year has rushed by and it hardly seems 51 weeks since we sat down to compose our last letter. We hope to get this out in time to reach most of you by Christmas, though abroad we fear it will be too late.

As I write Philip and Becca are at a meeting of the local Youth Group of the United Nations Association which doubles up usefully as an introduction to problems of world order and development and as a cosy youth club for the boys and girls from Withington Girls' School, MGS and other local schools. This afternoon they have been collecting old newspapers with a view to raising money for various good causes. Our professor of Greek was rash enough to offer the use of his garage for storage: now he can hardly get into it himself. Since Phillip is on the Sixth Form party circuit now Becca, as is often the way with the youngest, comes in for a fair amount of social life with him which she much enjoys.

Now that the regular household is reduced to four in term time and Rosemarie has decided to take a rest from the intensive academic work of the last two years we have had a larger than usual number of friends to stay. Stephen Burnett, now well in the saddle in charge of adult education at Church House, Westminster; Bill Pile, now permanent secretary at the DES; Mark Tweedy of Mirfield, who is stationed at the Royal Foundation of S. Katherine in Stepney; Gudrun Lerche, R's sister from Hamburg; Konrad Elsdon, now

common cultural heritage which still has some life in it. We shall be interested to see whether the course finds any takers.

Crispin comes home on Tuesday after his first term at Edinburgh, where he is reading Russian and Chinese. His Russian grounding at MGS seems to have been good enough to give him some leeway and allow him to concentrate on the intricacies of Chinese as well has having spare time for music and theatre. He leads the clarinets in the University orchestra and has bee assisting in Coriolanus production. The expedition to Persia about which we wrote last year was a great experience for him, not least the seven-day train journey each way. With Martin in Canada, Crispin in Persia, Philip in France to boost his command of the language for A levels, the family party at Calpe was reduced to three of us plus Becca's friend Jane. But we hope to make up for the all-directions summer by combining for a week's skiing at Obergurgl after Christmas.

Academic pressures are beginning to catch up with Becca now that O levels are coming up over the horizon. So far they don't seem to cause her more concern than they did to the boys. Music still bulks large and now that she occupies the 5th desk among the French horns of the Stockport Youth Orchestra (which for some reason is said to be vastly superior to its Manchester counterpart) she is getting good practice in ensemble playing. She and Jane ride out at Disley at weekends. Philip has become much interested in ballet through seeing the Northern Dance Theatre at work. As the tough guy of he family he doesn't seem to have much trouble keeping in trim and is put through his paces by one of the NDT's teachers once or twice a week. It remains to be seen whether the interest will be strong enough to take him to the Royal Ballet School at Barons Court at some stage.

Further instalments of one or two other stories begun last year; the search for a new Principal of the William Temple Foundation produced a strong short list from which Canon David Jenkins, formerly at Queen's, Oxford and currently in charge of the Human Study of the World Council in Geneva was selected. We much look forward to his arrival which should get the Foundation well under way in its new research and development role. The new theatre project for Michael Elliott and the 69 Theatre Company in the Royal Exchange is now well advanced with substantial support both from the Arts Council and the City fathers. Michael is moving up here to lead the enterprise full-time and has been doing an excellent job in getting everyone to pull together. So an opening in the autumn of 1974 seems quite feasible.

In the University the quinquennial settlement has been awaited with some anxiety. From the recent White Paper it looks as though things will be every bit as tight as we have feared. This is likely to dash EG's hopes for effective support at the tops of his Departments which have long outgrown the span of control of a single chair. Part of the problem is diversification. The new Centre for Educational Development Overseas of which he is chairman is already attracting a lot of demands since there seems to be no similar centre in the UK. The World Bank Study of Malawi is due for completion around the end of the year. Besides the Ford Foundation project he has been asked by the Commonwealth Secretariat to direct a series of seminars around the Commonwealth, which will require careful preparation during 1973 and 74. So we hope that some relief will emerge after all.

The 1973 letter

EG WAS FINISHING the Ford Foundation project on Broadcasting and National Development when he began his work in Brussels. The report published by McMillan's and the Harvard University Press, was particularly well received. It received the Book of the Year award of the American Association of Educational Broadcasters.

18 Cranmer Road,
Didsbury
Manchester 20

Second Sunday in Advent 1973

The shrinkage of the regular household which we reported last year would have reduced our numbers to two this autumn, but for the arrival of Grace Chokani from Zambia who spent a term with us while doing an advanced course at the Manchester College of Education. So Rosemarie and Becca had some reinforcement during the week, when EG was in Brussels. Grace, alas, goes home to her family at Christmas; we hope to have a young Greek postgraduate student to succeed her.

The spread of the family from Edinburgh to Mulanje in Malawi via Manchester, London and Brussels poses problems of communication, but it is surprising how much we manage to see of each other. Malawi is a bit far but EG may get there sometime in the New Year if Philip stays long enough. He arrived at the end of September, a few days after passing the driving test, a vital qualification for his work on the rural development project with which he is helping. The project combines the plentiful resources of labour in the villages at the foot of Mlanje Mount with quite limited Oxfam and other help in the way of water pipes and simple plumbing equipment. This combination provides an accessible and clean water supply to villages which up to now have had no more than distant and contaminated water holes. Philip spends most of the week in a caravan by the water intake a little way up the mountain and the weekends with Colin Glennie and his wife. His A-level Maths is coming in useful since he is coaching one of the Community Development Assistants with whom he works, for entry on 5 O-levels in the University of Malawi.

Martin returned from the USA early in the year having developed an interest in the work of the new neighbourhood law centres and legal aid for the disadvantaged generally. In order to be any use in this kind of work he has to be a professional and so he has decided to become a solicitor. It isn't at all easy to find a good firm with whom to serve the articles, so he was particularly pleased to be taken on by a very good firm in Gray's Inn who, besides all the usual things, have a strong practice in civil rights, consumer protection, the arts (Covent Garden, Sadlers Well etc) and literary matters. Having finished his probationary period he hopes to do a stint with the North Kensington Law Centre before beginning his course at the College of Law in Lancaster Gate in February. He and his friend Jane spent six weeks in Morocco in the summer and managed in that time to get across the Atlas range to the Sahara and West and North back up the Atlantic coast. It was their first experience of a non-European culture, just as Malawi is Philip's first. The younger generation are much less insulated against this impact than we were, both physically and psychologically. This enables them to respond more spontaneously and seems to do a lot for their views of the world, man and society.

Crispin spent six weeks in the summer in the USA with a group of other British undergraduates on a bursary provided by an American evangelical organisation. This turned out to be neo-Buchmanite and had the curious effect of making him appreciate the orthodox ministrations of the local Presbyterian church in upstate New York. He survived with the help of Frank and Eva Opton's hospitality, thus incidentally moving that family link into a new generation, a move which was reinforced by the visit of Frank and his Daughter Dorothy to Manchester in the autumn. Chris plods on with Russian and Chinese at Edinburgh. He has gone through Martin's car-owning phase and has discovered the same snags, except that it is now a good deal more with-it to decide to do without one than it was three years ago, so that he is likely to resort to pedestrian status that much sooner.

Becca's O-levels were average-plus and she copes as best she can with the absence of the boys. That is not too difficult since most of her own and Philip's circle of friends remains. The nucleus is still the UNA Youth Group, whose paper-recovery activities are becoming quite fashionable. Becca has also inherited Mrs Brown from the boys and visits her on Sundays. She is vice-captain of hockey and has moved up from the 5th to the 3rd desk among the horns in the Stockport Youth Orchestra. In the summer she spent a fortnight with some relations of friends in the Vosges whiles R and EG drove through southern France in search of a ruin. What we found was in fact a semi-ruined part of a little complex of farm buildings near the Dordogne river. With our usual reckless optimism we think that it could be repaired and turned into a family retreat without too much expense, becoming a second Starvecrow, this time in the sun. The Périgord countryside around is very restful and of course full of interest historically and archaeologically. Lascaux is about 15 miles away.

EG's translation to the EEC Commission in Brussels happened at fairly short notice and has been possible only because the University were prepared to give him leave and Derek Legge and Owen Ashmore were willing to carry the two departments in his absence. His departure coincided with the move of the Adult Education Department to larger premises in the Old Medical School and the consequent enlargement of the space available for the Extra-mural Department in the Roscoe building. EG is carrying on with the Ford Foundation project on Broadcasting and National Development. He and Michael Pilsworth, his research assistant, visited Nigeria in pursuit of this in October.

In Brussels he is Head of the Division concerned with employment and re-training matters in the directorate-general for social affairs. The commuting between Brussels and Manchester, though expensive, is easy: an hour or so on the plane and fifteen minutes at either end. So from Monday to Friday you can reach him in the office on 35.00.40, extension 1099 and on 35.71.77 at the family pied-a-terre in the Avenue de la Chevalerie (no.2) by the Parc Cinquantenaire. It would take another letter to say anything very meaningful about the European Commission. And in any case three months are too short a time for a balanced view. Perhaps twelve months hence it will be easier.

We sometimes think these letters are too optimistic and don't tell you enough about our troubles, failures and difficulties. Most of you know us well enough to be sure that we have plenty of all three. But at Christmas and the end of another year it is the things to be thankful about that tend to stand out, and perhaps this is no bad thing.

The 1974 letter

THE WORK IN the Adult Education Department identified the growing problem of youth employment. EG came to recognise that the move from one job to another in mid-career was one aspect of the Adult Education need. Another one was the actual insertion of young people into useful work at the end of their school career. This requires continuing education after the age of sixteen in an employment situation which has no clear definition of the jobs available to young people. So the Adult Education Department has in fact to deal with the early stages of further education, at a time when FE colleagues are themselves very much geared to preparation for specific jobs like plumbing etc. This letter also points to Philip's preoccupation with Africa. Reading African history at SOAS has reinforced his interest in the continent and we shall hear more about this as we go on. This letter is the first to mention our "ruin in Aquitaine" which Martin and Crispin were sent to France to find. It is interesting that forty years later, our house at Vigneau has become a substantial ingredient of our lifestyle. During 1974, the Manchester College of Adult Education also moved into a carefully designed new building on the Higher Education Precinct. EG had been much involved in its design which was unique in the country. As we shall hear later, the city council's decision to abolish the College and sell the building to the Polytechnic was a great blow to this distinguished institution.

18 Cranmer Road,
Didsbury
Manchester 20

Second Sunday in Advent 1974

As we look forward to Christmas this year we are particularly conscious of the world's need for the light and for the knowledge that the darkness shall not overcome it. The curious thing is that probably as much good is going on in the world as ever, but it is the troubles and suffering that get the attention. The news from Central and Southern Africa is probably more hopeful than it has been for many years, even if the first round of talks has not produced results. Elsewhere also old bonds of all kinds are being broken and new hope is springing up. R and EG were in Algeria in April in connection with the Ford Foundation Research Project and spent the Easter weekend in a sandstorm in the Ouargla Oasis on the edge of the Sahara. Since the plane to take us out could not land we were forced to stay on for the local fair-cum-folk-festival. It was fascinating to see how the new Algeria with housing estates and consumer goods is impinging on the age-old semi-nomadic existence of the people. Whether the new actually will prove to be better remains to be seen. But certainly the Algerian Fedayeen crowding into the Development Authority's stand seemed to think so. Our second visit in connection with the Project, to Malaysia, had to be postponed owing to the election there. Immediately after Christmas EG and his research associate, Michael Pilsworth, are off again to Tanzania and Sénegal.

R's preoccupations will keep her at home this time. Her work at the College of Adult Education in its spanking new building on the Higher Education Precinct flourishes. The Comparative Religion course is the only one on any theological subject in the College and is becoming an institution; as is the Manchester Inter-Faith Group which is now in its 6th year, bringing Muslims, Hindus, Jews, Buddhists and Christians together for what appears to be the only serious forum of discussion of matters of ultimate concern between the various religions in the City.

The problems of choice which are affecting so many of the young in our affluent society have included Martin and Crispin this year. Martin did his Part I exams for the Law Society and discovered in the process the aridity of the Law and the ambiguities of a lawyer's life. So for the present he is making chocolates instead with a little firm off Bond Street which aspires to a royal warrant since its double mints are said to be particularly appreciated by the Monarch. Crispin lost momentum in his Russian and Chinese studies at Edinburgh and is also intercalating at present. He shares a flat in the Dalkeith Road whence he contemplates Arthur's Mount, reads widely and takes and active part in the Edinburgh musical scene. The older generation did, I think, in some ways have an easier time, with little economic room for manoeuvre and imperatives which were as yet largely unquestioned.

Philip has just finished his first term at the School of Oriental and African Studies at London University, where he is reading African History and Swahili. His year in Africa has left its mark on him and has taken a good deal of digesting. He has been fortunate enough to get a room in Commonwealth Hall in Cartwright Gardens, so that he is within walking distance of SOAS and most other University institutions. Becca's job as captain of the hockey at Withington has been largely washed-out so far by the appallingly wet autumn. She and her contemporaries have been busy with their UCCA forms and are doing the rounds of the universities. Becca is attracted by Adam Curle's new Peace Studies course at Bradford. She is turning out to have a flair for driving with an instinctive feel for handling a car. With luck she will have her driving licence by Christmas.

Being plotted along the line from Edinburgh to Brussels the family meet at various times. The new Brussels flat (17 Ave. des Gaulois) can sleep more people than the last and provides a useful staging post, particularly in the summer and en route for the ruin in Aquitaine. The boys spent various periods down there to sort out what needs to be done and to help with the grape harvest.

Work in Brussels has been less paralysed than the papers would lead one to believe. There remain various areas of no progress in the Commission, but in many directions progress is possible. EG has been developing evaluation machinery for the European Social Fund and the new European Directive on equal Opportunities for Women. In recent months the hegemony of Latin styles of administration has experienced its first substantial challenge, after eighteen months of the British presence. Were we not operating on only three cylinders owing to the uncertainty about membership, I think we could begin to sort out some of the Kafka-esque absurdities of Commission procedure. These management problems are the keys to much that finds its way, quite unnecessarily, on to the summit agenda.

Whether we shall still be there next Christmas, who knows? Back in Manchester the University is getting impatient. The choice will not be easy.

The 1975 letter

IN THIS YEAR we learnt to cope with our membership of the European Common Market. EG was much settled in Brussels and became conscious of the need for sensible, low-key reform of the administrative procedures of the European Commission. EG was asked to stay at the Commission beyond the two year's leave of absence which the University had granted him. This means that he had to decide whether to abandon his established Chair in Manchester. In the event, it worked out well, and EG did not regret spending nine years in Brussels.

18 Cranmer Road,
Didsbury
Manchester 20

Second Sunday in Advent 1975

As we re-read last year's Christmas letter it seems that not much has happened, or at least changed, since Advent of 1974. The need for the Light is certainly as great. Mark Gibbs, in a manuscript sent for comment, writes 'this is a century of repression and torture, not a century of freedom'. In a sense he is right; and yet we can't help feeling that it is only part of the story. The South Moluccans sitting it out with their hostages in that train in Holland are after a freedom which they have never before had the chance to assert. So, presumably, are the IRA who are said to have planted the bomb (the 28th in the Belfast Europa) which EG missed by only a few hours in Belfast last week. In a sense it is all Woodrow Wilson's doctrine of national self-determination run riot. The new millenarianism, fed by totally unrealistic notions of individual and corporate autonomy.

On the other hand the Nine managed to sign the Lomé Convention with the forty-six developing countries: a not negligible document which recognises shades of poverty and ties the hands of the rich nations a good deal more tightly than any earlier agreement of this kind. And inspite of pockets of worsening destitution parts of the Third World are now beginning to take off. R and EG saw this in Singapore and Sumatra on the last of the country studies for the Ford Foundation project in April. The extent to which the prosperity of Singapore is shared is striking; in Sumatra the stunning beauty of the country and the comparatively solid agricultural base, as well as centuries of tradition, make development at best marginal, at worst amounting to vandalism. Fortunately Indonesian attitudes don't force the pace.

For both R and EG it was their first visit to the Far East. R brought back useful field experience for her World Religions course, which continues to grow. This year it began with the study of the religions produced by the first urban revolutions in ancient Egypt, Mesopotamia and the Indus valley, and then moved to the living religions of the Third World, particularly Hinduism, Buddhism and Islam. Just now they are grappling with the fascinating variety of insights and philosophical speculations of Hinduism and the capacity for openness and the adaptability of the Brahmans. The Interfaith group, having spent several years on the exploration of the theological world views of its members, has now moved on to the discussion of social and psychological issues. Its membership, like that of the theological coffee-party later to be called the Chantry Group, now in its 25th year, ebbs and flows.

The rest of the family are also at various stages of the way. When we are all at home we find ourselves increasingly ad idem about things that matter to us, which we enjoy. Martin, having helped to achieve a royal warrant for the mints about which we wrote last year, decided that chocolate making was too easy. So he joined the Office of Censuses and Surveys. As an Assistant Survey Officer he is a professional civil servant with all the perquisites of that condition, a fate he never envisaged but finds by no means worse than death. Since he helps to run the General Household Survey and other researches on which government policy is said to be based, he is discovering that the lead times involved usually mean that policy is changed just at the point at which the relevant evidence has become out of date.

He and Philip and their friends spent part of the summer painting at Vigneau, the ruin in Aquitaine which is slowly ruining us. Like all old houses it is fine until you begin tinkering with it. Then one wall needs to be rebuilt; the roof has to be re-tiled; the floor to be renewed, and so on. The local builders are voluble and persuasive. We are now trying to pay them off and do the rest ourselves.

Some young people are there for the winter and work their passage by a variety of jobs. Vigneau is a lovely spot, in fact the presbytère of a defunct church which long survived a village which, so our neighbour assures us as though it happened yesterday, was razed to the ground by the English. No prizes for the date of that one. We hope you will use it: it now has all mod cons and lots of room inside and out.

Crispin continues to intercalate by means of a variety of jobs and of none. His arguments against the rat race are cogent and ingenious, though R and EG wish he would not pursue them with the same energy that others devote to success. He is now thinking of going back to the university, possibly in Dublin next year. In the meantime his music continues to flourish. His performance of the *Weber Clarinet Concerto* at grandmama's 80th birthday party in March (a great omnium gatherum) was generally well thought of. And the New Orleans band which he and his friends mounted for Becca's 18th birthday party in the Octagon at Holly Royde in July was quite something.

Philip had a nasty fall while walking with friends in Scotland at Easter. The hospital at Oban thought little of it, but the orthopaedics at the MRI put his foot and ankle into hefty plaster for several weeks. He got back to his squash-dancing-swimming routine only in the autumn. He now shares Martin's flat and seems to have warmed a good deal both to Swahili poetry and to his first term of African history.

Becca did more than comfortably in her A levels and has an embarrassment of offers from universities for next October. In the meantime she is off to Germany after Christmas, having already 'done' Europe from the Channel to Athens and back on one of those season tickets in the summer. They saw Vienna, Rome, Dubrovnik and Venice en route, so it really was the journey of a lifetime. After Christmas she will be working at Bethel near Bielefeld, where Pastor Bodelschwingh created that remarkable set of institutions for the ill and disabled with which R's family have long been connected as doctors, architects and pastors.

Progress in Brussels is slow. The haphazard way in which the first (EG's) generation of officials from the UK were selected has, moreover, meant a rough weeding out since the referendum. So Paddy Hillery, his Commissioner, asked EG to stay on for a bit. This could only be done by giving up his full-time chair in Manchester: not an easy decision at all. Time will tell whether it was worthwhile. It is essential for some of the structural faults of the European edifice to be put right. But this demands the type of consistent application over a long period that is almost unknown in the Commission. Whether the next president, who is likely to be either Chrisopher Soames or Roy Jenkins (it being Britain's turn), will be prepared to face this?

In the meantime the family axis between Manchester and Brussels will continue to function. R will continue her work at the College and EG hopes to have a bit of time, once the Ford volume is out of the way, for the odd piece of work in the University. In the New Year he and Ghita Ionescu are starting a Graduate Seminar on European Social Policy, in which they hope to tackle some of the issues for which there is never enough time in Brussels.

The 1976 letter

BY THE TIME our Christmas letter fro 1976 was written, Rosemarie and I were living in a lovely flat on the Avenue Louise, which we occupied for the following six years. Following Becca's move to Sussex University. Rosemarie was able to join EG in Brussels. As luck would have it the Anglican chaplain in Brussels did not feel himself qualified to undertake the non Roman Catholic religious instruction at the European School. So he was glad to ask Rosemarie to do it. In September of '76, she became Professeur de Religion Protestante for the secondary school, provided for the children of European officials. Crispin, having abandoned his University education, required a lot of movement for ourselves and him, between Manchester and Brussels. Vernon Thomas moved into Cranmer Road with him, and was a great support to Crispin at this difficult time.

335 Avenue Louise
1050 Brussels
Belgium

Second Sunday in Advent 1976

As the address indicates our Christmas greetings this year come from what the Bruxellois like to call the capital of Europe. In fact we are finding Brussels a very liveable middle-sized town with a lot of attractive parts and the forest of Soignes almost on our doorstep. One of the most European things about it are the countless office blocks built by Jones, Lang and Wootton in the heady years around our entry and now largely unlet. Foreign investors have managed to destroy a good deal of the charming fin de siècle housing and the locals are only now beginning to fight back.

In September we moved into this larger flat half way between the Berlaymont and the European School, where R is now 'professeur de religion protestante' for the English secondary children. We have two researchers in

7. Rachel Heath & Molly Turner at Ty Pererin (the Pilgrim's House) in South Wales.

8. Tom & his Mother Maggie at Calpe, Spain with Grandma Rosemarie, 2002.

9. Rosemarie in Nanjing, a guest of Bishop R.H. Ting.

10. Rosemarie cycling in Beijing, 1989.

11. Braving hippos on the Zambesi in Zambia, 1988.

12. On the Nile at Luxor with David & Patricia Hughes, 1975.

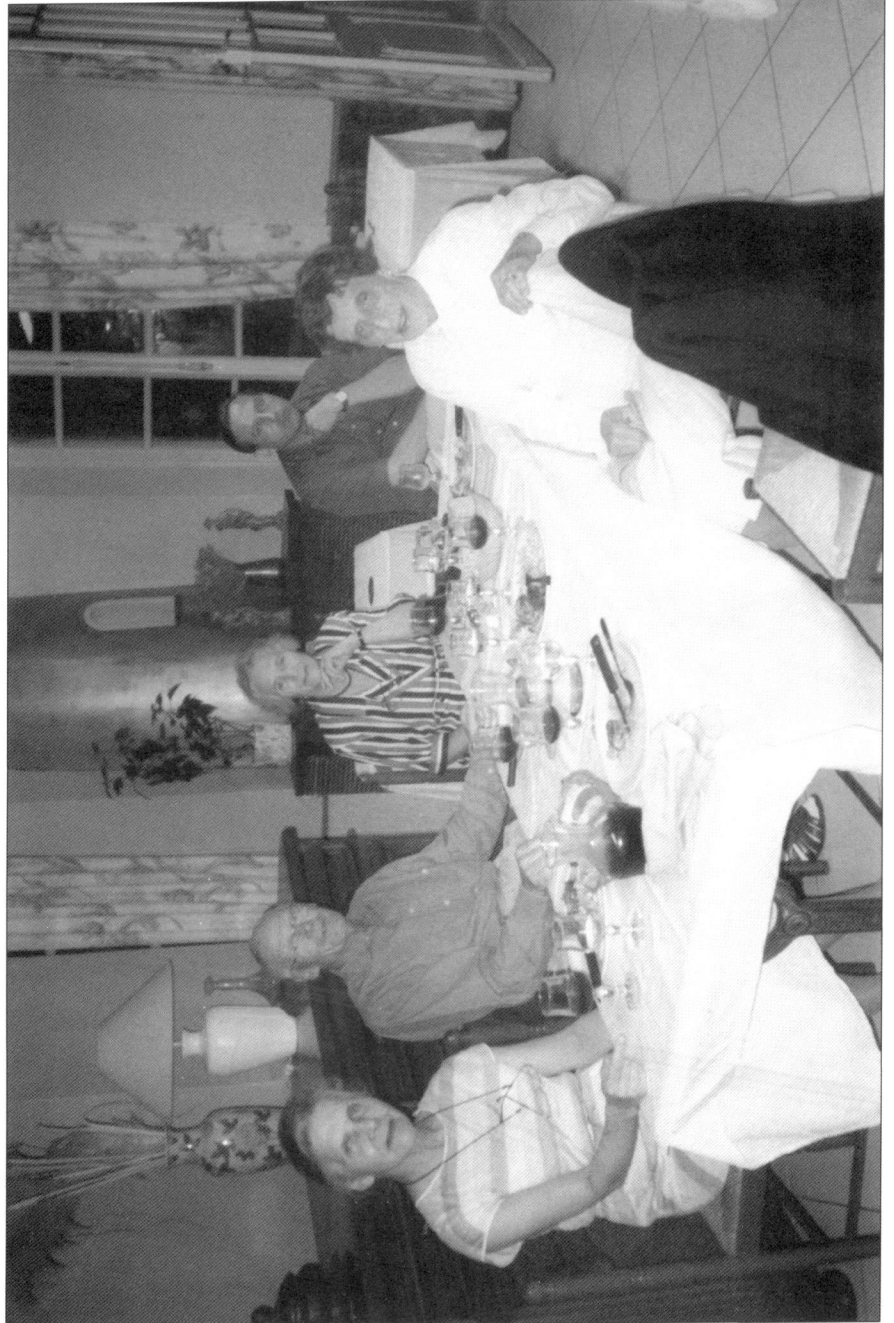

13. *Dinner at the Vieux Porlche with the senior Luykens & Gudrun, 1995.*

Cranmer Road, where we keep the attic and the study for our own use. Mrs Shepherd and Len look after house and garden as conscientiously as ever.

Being here at weekends enables us to get to know, if not the Belgians, at least the local expatriate community better. Its stratification deserves a PhD thesis: there are the veterans of Eurocontrol (who prevent aircraft from colliding) which was set up in 1960. Then there are the NATO officials, who came here on expulsion from Fontainebleau. And then there are the Eurocrats, some of whom have been here for twenty years and have built up a village-like network of their own. Holy Trinity Brussels is an interesting example. It is crammed to the doors every Sunday with an Anglo-American congregation of every shape and size and churchmanship. The service reflects the diversity and must cause the founding fathers of the Colonial and Continental Church Society to rotate in their graves. And yet this ethno-linguistic religion is a good deal more vital than much of its home based equivalent.

Rosemarie enjoys her work, though the change from teaching adults to coping with lively 11-year-olds and upwards is a bit exhausting. She continues to be surprised by the narrow sectarianism of those children who come from church-going homes. So she tries to broaden their religious base by a proper understanding of the Old and New Testaments and the growth of religious ideas. The school has about 3,000 children from the nine Member States and is one of eight such schools established wherever there are Community institutions. As may be expected, there are many structural, social and cultural problems, which the staff of about three hundred have only recently begun to tackle jointly, beginning with a two-day conference. So R feels she may have arrived at an important point in the life of the school.

Becca is still at Bethel and looking after three badly handicapped children. She went for five months, but has become so interested in her work that she arranged with Sussex to defer her admission for a year. She spent part of the summer working in a holiday camp at St Tropez and after a family party at Vigneau travelled round Spain with Judith. Philip worked on his project at Lamu off the Kenya coast during the summer vac and was lucky to get home alive from various reckless adventures. He is well into his third year at SOAS and runs a cheerful ménage in the flat which he shares with Martin, Stella and two other friends. The Census Office seems to suit Martin more than he cares to admit. He's much involved in a survey on surgical footwear at present, as well as editing the Christmas issue of the Department's house journal. EG is much reminded of his early days in the then Min of Ed, where one of his first jobs was to estimate the cost of eliminating earth closets in Cheshire village schools! Crispin's pilgrimage continues and he is just home after the autumn term back in Edinburgh. The way ahead is by no means clear as yet, though becoming less opaque.

EG is much occupied at present with the passage through the various Community institutions of a legal instrument to improve vocational preparation for the lower ability end of the school leavers. Since they tend to have the greatest difficulty when jobs are scarce and to be least qualified to get into the further education system, they lose out on every count. The hope is that Member states may do something if they can get some help from the Social Fund. Employment policy generally occupies a lot of his time, the more so since the medium term outlook has become politically recognised. It is surprising how little systematic work has been done in this field by the post-war generation. From his honorary chair at the Manchester Business School EG hopes to encourage some development work.

The general scene in Brussels has not changed much during the year. We were pleased that one of our predictions for the new president of the Commission proved to be correct. Great things are hoped for when Roy Jenkins arrives: it would be sad if the hope now were to be disappointed in the same way as the hope which accompanied our entry four years ago. There appears to be every intention to do a good job, both in the Commission and during the Council presidency, which falls to the UK for the first six months of 1976; not to mention the chairmanship of the Economic and Social Committee to which Basil de Ferranti was elected last month and the chairmanship of the Parliament, to which Scott-Hopkins has a good chance of succeeding in the New Year. So 1977 could be a good year in this respect.

The 1977 letter

ROSEMARIE AND I were able to undertake together many of my European missions during 1977. EG had to address a UNESCO regional conference on youth unemployment in Venice earlier in the year, another duty trip to Rome enabled us to spend a long weekend exploring Rome. Rosemarie had a tussle with some fundamentalist parents who thought her approach to the RE syllabus was too broad. She emerged from this skirmish much the stronger and never looked back. The arrival of Royal Jenkins as the President of the Commission should have introduced determined efforts to clean out the Augean stables in the Commission. In the event British interests during the UK presidency were too particular to leave much energy for that. EG's Visiting Chair in Employment Policy at the Manchester Business School enabled him to launch a modest programme on the actual use of human resources in industry at the School. This was a useful corrective to the overly finance-oriented teaching at the School.

335 Avenue Louise
1050 Brussels
Belgium

Advent Sunday 1977

I think I will make a start on this letter before driving out to the airport to meet Rosemarie who has been to Manchester to see Crispin. Since autumn has only just begun to turn into winter, the Christmas preparations have caught us unawares. Apart from everything else we have been unusually peripatetic since the summer. Our most recent joint trip was to Venice where a UNESCO regional conference on Youth unemployment required a paper from EG. It was R's first visit; EG had not been for fifteen years or so. We are happy to report that Venice is still above the water line and does not look in immediate danger. This is not to say that the danger is not real and that the effort to keep the city safe is not as vital as it has ever been. It is a magical place. On the Sunday we took a boat to the islands in the northern lagoon Murano, Burano and Torcello. The cathedral there, now surrounded by a handful of houses only, is having its mosaics restored and is already breathtaking in its beauty. Early November provided us with two marvellous days and two days of fog: in the end the only way out was by way of Trieste.

Earlier in the year we took advantage of another duty trip to Rome to spend a log weekend exploring the city. Unfortunately Patrick McLaughlin was not yet back there, but some friends of his took us to the Alban Hills end, by chance, to Nemi, the scene of the latest Muriel Spark novel. So we are gradually making up for our earlier neglect of Italy.

In Brussels Rosemarie is now well established at the European School. She emerged from a skirmish with some fundamentalist parents much the stronger, since she actually had some experience of religious education in England. She has now evolved a formula of cooperation with the local Anglophone clergy which encourages them to come in from time to time while leaving the professional responsibility to her. In a setting where clerical control of religious education has been up to now that is no mean feat. The RE periods have now been moved to the afternoon. This has the advantage of giving us a more leisurely start to the day, but of course the children are more tired towards the end of the school day and need more 'animation' if they are to take a real interest in their work.

Having become an established civil servant Martin decided to do a job abroad before, as he puts it, he gets too old! So he and Stella went out to Nairobi in the summer for a two-year teaching job at the Aga Khan High School there. They are the only Europeans in a mixed Asian/African School with a high opinion of its own excellence. A new headmaster is trying to broaden the curriculum and modernise the teaching and presumably M and S are intended to be part of this process. After their somewhat bohemian existence in London they now find themselves housed in a substantial house and garden with a queue of people anxious to join their domestic staff. The two-nations aspect of most African economies is particularly acute in Kenya and neither Martin nor Stella finds it easy to identify a stance which is both practicable and morally defensible. But they are fully engaged, and that is the main thing. In the cause of getting the school film projector to work (shades of Malawi) Martin is even becoming a bit of a film technician.

Philip is now the only member of the family left in the Acton flat, a circumstance which has taken a bit of getting used to. He was with us at Vigneau at Easter and spent the whole summer on various farms in Herefordshire and

Worcestershire. There is no doubt that country life suits him best: it will be interesting to see how he combines this with Swahili and African History when he finishes at SOAS next June. In the meantime he and Becca are within striking distance of each other, now that Becca has started at Sussex. She found it a wrench to leave Bethel after more than eighteen months' close involvement with her multi-handicapped charges. Torsten, one of them, came to stay with us again just before she went up. One consequence of her experience has been to make her change to Developmental Psychology. That course is much oversubscribed, so she may not be able to begin officially until next October. In the meantime a year reading some history and literature will do no harm. Apart from this upheaval life at the university seems to suit her. She fences and is learning to cope with Martin's ancient Morris Traveller which, he is sure, will have reached vintage status by the time he gets back.

Crispin's condition culminated in a serious nervous breakdown in the early autumn. Fortunately he decided to put himself in the care of one of EG's old colleagues in the Manchester Medical School, who has taken a great deal of trouble. Crispin is now much better and is thinking of working at the Royal Exchange Theatre under Michael Elliott for a while. He may take over Cranmer Road since our present tenant is thinking of buying his own house, and may share it with two or three other people.

He and we have been much blessed with our Manchester friends during these months when R and EG reverted to commuting between Manchester and Brussels at weekends. Vernon and many others not only held the fort in between but also fed, watered, sheltered and encouraged us.

On the European front progress has been slower than we hoped this time last year. The British presidency of the Council was not an easy one: there were too many issues on which HMG felt strongly. This made it difficult for the British minister concerned to be impartial in the chair. Rather too much was made of this by those who wanted to have the UK's half-heartedness confirmed. Whatever the fair interpretation, it did make Roy Jenkins' first six months difficult. Now there is the argument about the means of achieving economic and monetary union and RJ's bold, but somewhat quixotic, bid for a leap forward. At a time when three pretty backward countries are applying to join and will need massive transfers of resources from the better off members, this does not seem vastly realistic. EG's own preoccupation is mainly with unemployment. He has been trying to persuade ministers that only a substantial application of the community service volunteer principle can bother put some of the 2 million young unemployed to work and meet the many un-met needs in all communities. This seems at long last to be sinking in. 1978 may well see an EEC initiative in this field, and not a moment too soon.

R wants to add that the earlier reference to her cooperation with the clergy does not mean that she is not pursuing the Comparative Religion interest. She has Hindus, Muslims and Jews taking part in the RE programme, some of which is shared with the Roman Catholic stream. Altogether that side of life at the European School seems to be very lively and worthwhile.

The restoration of Vigneau is getting on. Having planted a hedge at Easter, we arranged for the grass round the house to be cut regularly while we were away. This did wonders for the meadow and the croquet. Various Manchester and other friends used it in the course of the year. While we were there in the summer we discovered a local music school-cum-festival and countless musical occasions in the neighbouring churches and castles. It seems that most French musicians migrate south in July and August and enjoy themselves making music on holiday. The mix of amateur and professional music is quite unselfconscious and surprising in a country like France. Just before Christmas a young Australian couple will be moving in for a few months and will, we hope, do some decorating and planting of fruit trees.

The 1978 letter

THE CHRISTMAS LETTER refers to women priests in Denmark, well before we started ordaining women in the Church of England. At that time I was already a member of the first Committee created to promote the ordination of women to the Anglican ministry. Rosemarie's concern at the time was the dialogue between the different faiths. She was much involved with the World Congress of Faiths. Martin was still with Stella, his then-girlfriend, and they were working for the Aga Khan's School in Nairobi. Rosemarie and I had probably the most spectacular holiday on the Indian Ocean in Kenya while snorkelling in the Pemba Channel off the Kenya Coast.

335 Avenue Louise
1050 Brussels
Belgium

Advent Sunday 1978

We look forward, after two years away, to spending Christmas at Cranmer Road again this year. Since the beginning of the academic year Crispin has been joined there by two postgraduate students and the new assistant stage manager at the Royal Northern. And as most of them will be away over the holidays, we can have the house for our use. So we hope to see something of our friends and neighbours.

The year in Brussels has been pretty arduous as far as the Commission in concerned. The relationship of input of effort to output of discernible results has been worse than usual. One of the hazards of operating in our type of activity is that there is an election in the offing somewhere almost all the time. This makes at least one Member State (or rather its government of the day) reluctant to move in any direction lest some voters take umbrage. This time last year we hoped to do something substantial to help those countries with serious youth employment problems. The intervention of the French elections set us back almost twelve months. The UK elections in 1979 will have much the same effect and, I think, the German will do much the same in 1980. From this point of view alone it will be a boon to have a single date for European elections (give or take the gap between a Thursday and a Sunday).

But the year also had more cheerful moments. The best of them for R and EG was their visit to Kenya at Easter to see Martin and Stella. For R it was the first trip to East Africa and the country lived up to its reputation for contrasts. Parts of Nairobi elegant and mid-atlantic; others, just beyond Martin's house in Westlands, as much a shanty town as ever. Some excellent roads; all but impassable and tracks elsewhere. On the eastern flanks of Mount Kenya we twice found ourselves literally bogged down. EG had manfully refused the loan of the EEC delegation's four wheel drive vehicle and wished he had been less scrupulous. But someone with a landrover passed by in due course and pulled us out. We spent a night by the Waso Nyiro river in the Northern Region of the Samburu tribe. In some ways the unexpected high light was, however, a swim among the fantastic fish and coral off Kisite Island in the Pemba Channel on the Tanzanian frontier. Even the author of the guide book had never managed to get out there.

Philip was glad to come to the end of his time at the School of Oriental and African Studies, did reasonably well in his finals and went back to his farming in Herefordshire from the beginning of the strawberry seasons to the end of the hop-picking. He is now getting experience with livestock on a farm in Norfolk. He works from 7.30 to 6pm and has only every other weekend off. So, as he writes, it's a good thing I enjoy it. He and Lindsey, who teaches nearby, have found a comfortable flat in the country near Norwich.

We celebrated Becca's twenty-first just before the summer holidays and a good time seems to have been had by all. Martin contributed his by now customary verses. The only problem was to decide who had come in fancy dress and who merely looked as though they had. So Elizabeth Curling's punk outfit was mistaken for the real thing and the prize went to Cathy Wedell's very professional outfit as a member of the Olympic Sleeping Team. Becca did manage the transfer to the Developmental Psychology course earlier in the year. This is hard work both in terms of theory and of the mechanical skills needed, such as a reasonable statistical background. She had to move out of the Park Village for the second year, but lives quite pleasantly in the top half of a house only just behind the Brighton seafront with three other girls.

Crispin moved from the Royal Exchange Theatre to the University Library just after Easter After a spell as a porter he was appointed to the issuing desk in September. He is by no means convinced that he wants to make his career in library work, but for the time being this provides a friendly and congenial job.

R, while writing her contribution, is listening to one of her musical discoveries: *Rachmaninov's songs* sung by Elisabeth Söderström accompanied by Ashkenazy. What a thrilling voice and beautiful music. The other find was Schubert's Wanderer fantasy, one of his last piano sonatas, which comforts and moves the soul. The second year at the European School has been one of consolidation and progress. R is well enough established to bring her own ideas to bear on the RE teaching. The Dutch, Danes and British continue to work together well and last week the seventh year took part in a discussion with the Danes about infant/adult baptism. Incidentally they learnt that half the theological students in Denmark are women, women have been ordained for thirty years and the president of the synod is a woman.

R's other concern is, of course, the dialogue between the different faiths Her older pupils respond well to the concept of religious pluralism. In July she arranged the first ever inter-faiths dialogue held in Belgium. Pupils, parents and teachers as well as members of five world religions took part. Becca was asked to write an account of it for the British journal of the *World Congress of Faiths*, which will also contain R's impression of the Congress' annual conference in York in September. So there is much to be thankful for, and hopeful about not least the ongoing discovery of the Christian contribution and role within the religious experience of mankind.

Martin and Stella appear to be involved in the way in which modernisation in Kenya affects their African friends individually. One of them was wrongfully imprisoned and they experienced the problem of securing him justice; another has little hope of raising the £300 needed to buy her own shamba. At school the effectiveness of his 'fun' approach to learning English is about to be tested by the examination results which make or mar the future opportunities of the African (as distinct from the Asian) children. Having seen off a colleague with a goat-roasting in their garden, they plan to spend Christmas in an attempt to reach at least one of the peaks of Mount Kenya.

Broadcasting in the Third World, which Harvard published in the US and MacMillan in England, has had a very kind reception from the critics, and has just been given the Book of the Year award by the National Association of Educational Broadcasters in America. It is a sobering thought that it is the moderately thorough research design that has attracted most critical acclaim: something that one should be able to take for granted as a sine que non of social research. Coming as it did just before the UNESCO quarrel about freedom of information there is a fair amount of interest in such proposals as we felt able to make. The notion of 'reasonable distance' between government and the broadcasters appears to ring a bell, though it is not easy to put this into institutional terms.

Vigneau has been in use for all but four or five weeks during the year; so we were able to finish the work on the back of the house. Di and Joe Rundus did wonders with the painting inside and out before moving to Cranmer Road to have their baby, and then back to Australia; Now there are some New Zealanders, followed by a German family. From March to July there are several gaps as well as later in the year. So do announce yourselves.

The 1979 letter

R EVIEWING OUR 1979 Christmas letter from 2012, it is melancholy to recognise that I heard for the first time out loud that it might be best for the British to pull out of the European Community, so our shilly-shallying has been going on for over thirty years. The curious inability of all our governments to recognise that European unity is something that has to be worked for is pathetic.

335 Avenue Louise
1050 Brussels
Belgium

Advent 1979

Advent this year seems to be beset with a particularly intractable group of problems on the political scene: the harrowing ordeal of the hostages in Teheran, the last-minute failure of the Zimbabwe-Rhodesia negotiations and the unresolved row about the UK's contribution to the EEC budget. Mobility makes for interdependence, and interdependence seems to require an ever-increasing degree of consensus. So the mainstream of movement can be held up indefinitely by a minority of dissentients. One's reaction depends on whether one thinks of that as a sign of advancing civilisation or not!

We here are affected directly only by the last of these problems. At the local BBC office the other day EG for the first time heard someone say out loud that it might perhaps be best for the British to pull out, if they really found it all so unpalatable. Curiously that seems to be the last thing the government have in mind. And the new Tory Euro-MP's certainly behave as though they meant to stay in Strasbourg for a long time. Indeed, all British MEP's have quickly become plus *royaliste que le roi*. Their disgust at Mr Walker's turnabout on dairy pries (i.e. his agreeing to their increase in the face of all the evidence) produced an agonised letter from EG's colleague Stanley Johnson in *The Times*:

he would never again, he said, be able to look his electors in Hampshire in the eye. If all this leads to the assertion by the European Parliament of the interests of the ordinary citizen of the Community the present travail may yet in retrospect come to be seen as a time of growth.

The family are much spread out this Christmas. Martin and Stella, after another good year in Nairobi, think it is time to disengage from their work at the Aga Khan School. They plan to spend Christmas in Abu Dhabi with a friends of Martin's, then to go on to India for some months before returning home around mid summer for some postgraduate training next October. Martin seems to have discovered his didactic talents and wants to validate them with a teaching diploma. He is waiting to hear whether Macmillans like his English course sufficiently to want to publish it.

Crispin came to Brussels in the spring and started at the Royal Conservatoire in October. He hopes to do the Clarinet Diploma and then perhaps to settle in Edinburgh. In the meantime he plays in the Conservatoire orchestra and in the Philharmonie Royale d'Ottignies, which his professor conducts. His friend Maria is a great support, particularly since his health is still very uncertain and his condition varies from week to week.

Philip is on his way to Kenya overland and hopes to get there before Martin and Stella leave. He finished his contract with the cows in Norfolk and spent the summer back with the Middletons and the Clifts on the Welsh border. Now he wants to have another look at East Africa before deciding what to do with himself.

The death on Good Friday of EG's mother as a result of a heart attack was mercifully swift and painless. She was just eighty-four and had only recently begun to find life really burdensome. Her ten years at Haus Loerick had been in many ways a very fruitful coda to her life. As one of the founder members of the community she was still able to take a lively part in the shaping of its life. She was buried in the family grave in Düsseldorf after an Anglo-German funeral service taken by Ernst Rocholl and Harold Lockley.

R and EG spent Holy Week in Israel. The purpose of the visit was to meet Interfaith groups there. We started with a two-day stay at a Christian kibbutz in Northern Galilee founded by the Dutch Reformed Church in the 1960's. Since it was also the Jewish Passover we took part in a memorable Seder when the Jews remember the Exodus. The liturgy had been fashioned around the meal and consisted of readings and prayers from the Jewish Passover and Christian Maundy Thursday services. After EG had left R stayed on a the convent of the Sisters of Zion in the Old City of Jerusalem. From there she made contact with two more groups: the Hope Centre founded by one of the Sisters of Zion and devoted to the Jewish-Christian-Muslim dialogue; and Windows to the East led by Father Murray Rogers, formerly an Anglican missionary in India. Here there are weekly meditations after the Buddhist manner which provide a necessary balance in their reminder of the religions of the Far East.

Elihu and Ruther Katz introduced R to the beautiful new city outside the walls and took her to a concert and the Book Fair where Isaiah Berlin received the 1979 prize for his work for peace. We felt (EG again) that one can understand the complexity of the relationship between the three faiths of the Holy Land only be being there and sharing the country's life.

May brought on the European elections in which EG stood as Liberal candidate for the nine Westminster constituencies making up the Euro-constituency of Greater Manchester West. It was a sobering experience, though in human terms very rewarding. By dint of three weeks' hard work we reckoned to have persuaded about five thousand people who would not otherwise have done so to vote Liberal. The result, with David Steel's help on the Eve of Poll, was the only saved deposit in the area.

In June Becca heard that she had been awarded one of the Sussex University exchange scholarships to the United States. So she has been at Occidental College, Los Angeles since September. Since the year there is a bonus, she can afford to do a lot of music and other things besides Psychology. She plans to spent Christmas in Mexico with a friend from Sussex.

The 1980 letter

THERE IS AN interesting reference to the visit by Neil Tyler and his Daughter Mariot (my god daughter) to Vigneau. My recent researches on behalf of the Chantry Group show that Mariot and her Brother Piers are still in touch with us, even though they no longer agree with their father's Christian perspectives. Rosemarie's links with the Institute for the Comparative Study of Religion in Antwerp began that year, and has lasted until now when the Institute has started a fund in memory of her, to help students wishing to study there.

335 Avenue Louise
1050 Brussels
Belgium

Second Sunday in Advent 1980

We are a week behind with our Christmas greetings because EG has only just returned from one of his missions to Portugal where he has been putting in hand some EEC aid for their human resource development. We hope none the less that this letter reaches you on time.

This year has flown. For the family it has been one of home comings. Martin and Stella came back overland from India and arrived on foot in Vigneau in August; Becca flew in to Ostend from Los Angeles one night in July; and Philip hitchhiked from Athens in September after six months in a Kibbutz in the Galilee. So we hope to be all together for Christmas for the first time in four years.

In Brussels Crispin and Maria and her two small girls moved into a bigger flat with a little garden in Woluwe St Pierre (address: 295 rue Francois Gay, 1150 Brussels) in September. This gives them more room both for Tina and Griet to run about and for Crispin to develop his clarinet teaching. His health is a good deal better (though there is a fair way to go yet), and he has been able to take on four pupils in addition to his work at the Conservatoire. For this we are more grateful than we can say to all our friends here and in England who have supported him and us so faithfully during these past years.

As a result of her encouragement of interfaith contacts in Belgium R has been appointed a trustee of the new Institute for the Comparative Study of Religions. The Institute received its royal charter in June and the first courses began in October. R herself is preparing a course on the cross-fertilisation and diffusion of religious ideas for the next academic year. This quest of hers also found a lively echo with an Anglo-German-Dutch group of the Blue Pilgrims whom we much enjoyed having here in May. At the same time R continues to be much taken up with her teaching at the European School and likes the contact this gives her with the young. We both support the Ecumenical Centre when we can, particularly with a group of Economist EC officials who try to do their work in a Christian perspective.

Over Easter we had a fortnight in Crete following the Minoan trail in the footsteps of Schliemann and Arthur Evans. Sitting at Phaestos on one of those superb days when the air shimmers with colour and light was a timeless experience. Knossos also is fascinating, particularly when seen in the context of that exciting account of Evans' work in *The Bull of Minos* (by Leonard Cottrell). The Cretans themselves are most hospitable, especially those living off the beaten track. In a monastery on the Lasithi plateau we made friends with Sister Irene who looks after the three remaining 'papas' and plied us with coffee and, alas, largely incomprehensible, conversation.

At Vigneau in the summer the house was full most of the time. Bob and Andrea Leaf, David and Patricia Hughes, Oleg and Genia Pomerantzoff plus Andrew and a cousin, Neil Tyler and EG's god-Daughter Mariot, Becca and her American friend Christine, Crispin and Maria and Martin and Stella came and went. Neil with his botanical expertise was able to name the Chusan palms and other flora that we had never identified. At present the house is occupied by a group of archaeologists whose iron-age dig near Killliekrankie has closed down for the winter.

Martin and Stella are at Cranmer Road. He is at the university to do his postgraduate teaching course which in Manchester one can double up with the Diploma in Teaching English Overseas. His English textbook is in the press with Macmillans. If the Kenya government decide to adopt it for the CPE he should be able to retire on the proceeds! Stella in the meantime is doing a teaching job and the household at Cranmer Road seems friendly and peaceful. EG tends to be in the University once a month, though he has not had much time for teaching this year. An article on the employment situation which the *MBS Review* brought out in July attracted some attention three or four months later as the government realised that something must be done to cope with the inexorable rise in unemployment. The notion of an integrated work/training period for all youngsters between the school leaving age and the end of the teens is gaining ground.

The time in Israel gave Philip some more practical experienced in the handling of livestock and dairying. He also saw a good deal of the country and came back with a sober assessment of life there. In the autumn he applied for the job of Assistant to the Director of Indian Boys Towns Trust and met Joe Homan, the Director, here during a fund-raising visit to Brussels. The Trust runs a series of rural settlements in the Madurai region of South India where boys and girls are trained for agriculture and agricultural processing along intermediate technology lines. Joe Homan is getting on and is looking for a potential successor. Whether this is the right medium term job for Philip remains to be seen. Initially he going out for a probationary period, probably in February.

R and Becca went to the States together last year and crossed the South by bus from Atlanta to LA, where Becca spent the year at Occidental College. She made the most of life in California, particularly on the music side. EG met her in New York in May en route to the World Communications conference in Philadelphia. So she saw something of New England and the Optons in their beautiful country retreat near Princeton. Now in her last year at Sussex life is fairly tough since most of the final exams consist of essay assessment throughout the year. The choice of a job afterwards is not going to be easy either. She could pursue something on the music/arts side or develop child psychology. We shall see.

The 1981 letter

THIS YEAR PHILIP was busy in India, and learnt to manage the training responsibility for farmers. This is a precursor of the Kaloko Trust which he established in Zambia a few years later. It is also the beginning of Becca's interest in the Community Arts movement, as a result of her work with the Laban Centre for Movement and Dance in London

335 Avenue Louise
1050 Brussels
Belgium

Advent Sunday 1981

Last year we avoided the political situation in our Christmas letter. But this year, like 1979, 'Advent seems to be beset by a particularly intractable group of problems'. Of those the Iran hostages are home and Zimbabwe is independent, though 'the row about the UK's contributions to the EEC budget' simmers on. Instead, the nuclear threat and the Middle East are on the boil again. But the fact that two of the issues that seemed insoluble two years ago were in fact resolved give us hope that the current issues will also become more amenable. As for the EEC budget reform, the London summit showed that a shared understanding of the problem is emerging. One has the feeling that the impact of the world recession on all Member States is making them more understanding towards each other. The Schmidt/Brezhnev meeting had a similar feel to it; and that may spill over to the Geneva talks. So we think we have much to be thankful for this Adventtide.

R had a fairly peripatetic year. Just before Easter she and her Sister Inge spent ten days in Russia. In Moscow they managed to visit the Vederonikovs and their Daughter Tanya. The first time the meeting was easy and they had instant rapport, Tania translating from the German into Russian and vice versa. On their second visit on their last evening in Moscow it was much more difficult to reach them. These two experiences seem typical of the situation. The warmth and vitality of the people and their achievements on the one hand. Watching them at their Saturday evening dinner dance in Kieve was tremendous fun. On the other hand one is aware of their isolation from, and ignorance of, the rest of the world, and their difficulty in getting food and consumer goods and in making contact with foreigners. It is true that the Church in Russia lives: the church in Kiev was full to overflowing with all age groups. R feels that such visits to Russia should be a must for all those who care about breaking down the barriers of distrust between the two extremes of Western civilisation. Europeans in the West should accept their responsibility for this.

In May R took about twenty fifth formers to Geneva for a week's study of international organisations: the UN, the Red Cross, CERN and the World Council of Churches. It was a most interesting time and she intends to take another group in 1982.

In August R was in Calpe, first with Jill Rose an then with EG who did the 'permanence' in the office for the first half of August. In early September they drove across the central and northern plateaus of Spain which are surprisingly well-developed and fertile. They crossed the Pyrenees at Roncesvalles where Roland of the Song lost his life in the battle against the Moors in the 12th century.

In Belgium R's work with the Institute for the Comparative Study of Religion, now housed in the new buildings of the University of Antwerp, is building up. She has seven mature students, two of them a convert Bahá'í and Muslim respectively. It is striking how all over Europe there is a breaking out from religious isolation and a recognition that we are becoming one of the multi-religious regions of the world.

Martin finished his Postgraduate Certificate as well as the TSL Diploma in the summer, having done his teaching practice in Lisbon in the spring. Macmillans brought out his English textbook for Kenya at long last. In the light of the job situation in the teaching profession he was lucky to walk into a post at the Blackburn Language Centre where they deal intensively with the language problems of immigrant children and young people. This is just the sort of experience he needs to add to his work in Kenya. He had a lucky escape when he was run into by a stolen car being chased by the police in Albert Square. The front half of his much-prized Morris Traveller had to be reconstructed but he escaped with shock and some bruises.

After two years at the Royal Conservatoire and a summer holiday with Maria in England Crispin decided to make music a hobby rather than a full-time occupation. In September he started work with Ernest Hochland at the University Booksellers in Manchester. The literary environment seems to suit him and Maria and the children like it in Manchester. So it is quite possible that they will settle there in the course of the next year or so. In the meantime they meet in Brussels, London or Manchester as and when they can afford it. Earlier in the year Cris and two friends from the Opera gave a chamber concert in aid of the Boys' Town Trust. They did the *Spohr Seven Songs* for Soprano and Clarinet which everyone liked a lot. Philip was very glad of the proceeds to enable him to put a perimeter fence round the settlement at Pannaikadu.

Pannaikadu is in the hills north-west of Madurai where Philip was put in charge of a new settlement intended to grow coffee and bananas on a 30-degree slope. He has learnt a lot about tropical agriculture as well as about human nature during this year, being thrown in at the deep end in terms of management responsibility. For the last three months he has been in charge of the whole enterprise while his boss was in England to raise funds and have a rest. Phil in turn is due to come home in January for two to three months to do the same. So he may be looking in on some of you.

Becca finished her Psychology degree at Sussex in June and applied for a place on the postgraduate course in Movement and Dance at the Laban Centre. This is housed at Goldsmiths' College in London. Since she has a lot of friends in Brighton by now and is very active in the Women's Movement there, she has kept her room there and commutes to New Cross in the week. At first she found the physical exercise very hard going, but by now she is well in training. It will be interesting to see what she makes of this combination of disciplines.

The deteriorating employment situation has been preoccupying EG and his colleagues in the Commission. After the best part of a year of preparation they now have a scheme which would enable the Commission to underwrite combined work/training schemes for the 16-18-year-olds who have no jobs. The implementation of this depends on changes in the Community budget. And this is where we came in.

The 1982 letter

I RESIGNED FROM THE Commission after nine years in order to make room for a senior Greek official, the Greeks having that year joined the European Community. I had gone to Athens before I retired to look into the unemployment situation in Greece. They told me that unemployment was two percent of the working population, at a time when it was eight or nine percent in the rest of the Community. I discovered that the reason for the low figure was that a large part of the Greek labour force consisted of subsistence farmers who did not pay any unemployment insurance and were therefore not counted in the official statistics.

18 Cranmer Road
Manchester
M20 0AW

Advent 1982

Here we are back at Cranmer Road after the best part of a decade in Brussels. Having for some time been uneasy about the modus operandi of the EEC Commission in general, and of the social policy area in particular, EG had been thinking of leaving the Commission. In the course of this year the opportunity occurred to 'disengage' (as distinct from retiring) in order to make room for a senior Greek official. This seemed a good opportunity to practice what EG had preached, i.e., that there should be much more mobility of people into and out of the European civil service. Rather than spend another ten years in a comfortable but unproductive job EG decided to take the opportunity to go.

R was in a rather different position since she was doing a very fulfilling job at the European School which might well have continued for another few years. So we faced the all-too-common dilemma of professional couples these days. We did consider taking a small flat from which R might continue her job

14. *EGW emphasising a point at a meeting of the EIM.*

15. *Sir Frank Roberts, EGW, Prime Minister Rau, Fransisco Balsemao and Princess Margaret of the Netherlands at the opening of the headquarters of the EIM in Düsseldorf, 1993.*

16. *Bryan Luckham & EGW at the Publication Party for* Television at the Crossroads, *2001.*

17. *Arrival at Ahmedebad at the Educational TV Channel, 2000.*

18. Princess Margriet of the Netherlands, President of the European Cultural Foundation with EGW at the opening of the EIM's building in Düsseldorf, 1993.

19. *Dame Mabel Tylecote, Professor Ross Waller, Owen Ashmore, the 'old guard' of Adult Education in Manchester.*

20. *Wyndham Place/Charlemagne Trust Party at 10 Downing Street. Mrs Blair was the hostess.*

and commute in the reverse direction. In the end she decided not to do that but to se the freedom from a regular job to travel more extensively and to do all those things for which there has been no time in the past.

Most of the autumn has been taken up with putting our house in Cranmer Road back into shape and to make a few structural improvements, such as putting another bathroom into part of Becca's old room and to replace the companion way to the top floor by a proper stairway. Now all is more or less in order. R is about to fly to South India to spend Christmas with Philip and to spend some time at one or two Ashrams. Since she was welcomed back with open arms at the College of Adult Education, she will be back in mid-February to take up her lectures on Comparative Religion again.

Martin has been in Riyadh (Saudi Arabia) since the beginning of November with Cable and Wireless Ltd who are carrying out a massive communications contract there. His part in the scheme is to provide ESP which these days doesn't mean what it used to mean. It stands, in fact, for English for Special Purposes and is a sub-system of EFL (English as a foreign language). His students are young communications technicians whose job will be to run and maintain the system once it is set up. Owing to the conditions of life in Riyadh Martin has home leave every four months; so we hope to see him from time to time.

Crispin is dividing his time between musical studies and part time work with social service agencies. As a visiting student in the Faculty of Music he can supplement the CGE course which he never took at MGS, being too busy with Russian, French and English. Maria and the children are at rue François Gay since Maria joined the European Standards Authority earlier in the year. Cris goes over from time to time.

Philip is doing a double stint at Tirumangalam and will not be home until next autumn. He was in England and Belgium for about two months in the spring, most of his time being taken up with lecturing and money-raising in the two countries. He is now in sole charge of three boys' towns where he is introducing new types of crops and intensive farming methods. He doesn't get away much, so he is always glad to have visitors, of whom there seems to be a steady trickle even in that out-of-the-way corner of the country.

The course at the Laban Centre for Dance and Movement seems to have opened up a new range of interests for Becca. She did well in her Diploma in July and is now working with a Community Dance project sponsored by the Lambeth borough council. It looks fairly precarious to us as far as economic security is concerned, though clearly very interesting as an attempt to enlarge the sensibilities of the local population. Becca is convinced that it will turn out a great success and that the borough council will show its appreciation in more tangible terms in six months' time. She still commutes from Brighton where she now feels well established.

The disengagement from Brussels has given EG the chance to return to his work on broadcasting policy and to develop this in a European context. This is turning out to be timely in view of the breaking down of national broadcasting policies in the face of the imminent arrival of direct broadcasting by satellite, the sudden revival of interest in cable systems of all kinds, and the sudden penetration of videocassettes. The University, in cooperation with the European Cultural Foundation in Holland, is establishing a European Institute for Communication to tackle the policy implications of all this. EG is to be the Institute's director. Given the economic situation it takes a little time to provide a firm foundation for the Institute. Quite recently that has emerged, and a formal launching will be held early in the New Year.

The 1983 letter

HAVING SETTLED IN Manchester, our life returned to its pre-Brussels tenor. This was the age of Rosemarie's extended travels to India, China, and later Zambia. It was also the year of Rachel Heath's death, whose friendship with our family extended over forty years and three generations. Our links with her were close, particularly during our years at Starvecrow, our house near Sevenoaks.

18 Cranmer Road
Manchester
M20 0AW

Advent 1983

It seems next to no time since we sent you the 1982 letter. At that time we were still resettling in Manchester. In the last twelve months life has taken on once more much of the tenor it had before we moved to Brussels. R goes to the College of Adult Education to teach her Comparative Religion Class on Monday mornings and to keep up with her French on Fridays; EG goes off to the University much as he used to. And yet we seem to have come back from Brussels with a European 'formation' which colours a lot of our judgments and activities. We go back and forth quite a lot: R to the 25th anniversary celebrations of the European School in October and an Interfaith dialogue organised by her Brussels friends earlier in the year; EG to develop the relations of the new European Institute for the Media (which is flourishing) with a variety of EEC and other European agencies.

The counterflow also is lively. Since most of the planes from Amsterdam, Brussels, Paris etc., tend to arrive early, our colleagues attending Institute meetings come to breakfast and a lot of outstanding questions are settled by half past nine.

This year both Martin and Philip have been in and out as well. Martin on his four-monthly leaves from Riyadh and Phil during his home leave in the autumn. Most of Phil's time has in fact been spent on the road; he can't remember how many meetings he has addressed for the Boys Town Trust, but he has been to Truro at one end and to Tyneside at the other end of the country. Next Sunday he goes back East, this time as field director for Sri Lanka (which for some reason seems a good deal more accessible than Tirumangalam). His work there, both in terms of agricultural development and in systematising the administration of the Trust's work, seems to have gained much more recognition in the last year. He hopes to apply the same principles in Sri Lanka for another two years.

Martin's contract with Cable and Wireless has been extended to the middle of 1984. In spite of the extraordinary difficulties one seems to encounter in trying to get to know the Saudis as people he seems to have made some lively contacts outside the expatriate circle, and to be getting to know the Arabian peninsula. He has brought back some spectacular photography and sends hair-raising accounts of sand yachting expeditions.

Crispin is in the middle of the A-level Music course after getting an A in his O-level in the summer. He has decided to read musicology in the Music Faculty either here or elsewhere rather than go for a performer's qualification. But his planning goes on; he leads the clarinets in the Gorton Philharmonic and recently gave a chamber concert with Patricia Whiting and Alison Read-Jahn in aid of Nancy Hoare's (alias Sister Anna) Lagan College Appeal. Nancy came over for it, in great form and having just come back from a fund-raising tour of the United States. In the continuing tragedy of Northern Ireland the Lagan experiment of educating Catholic and Protestant children together seems to us to be one of the signs of hope.

Dance continues to dominate Becca's life as she commutes between Brighton and London. Her most recent exercise in choreographing and dancing as a group activity has just been put on videotape, and the rest of the family hope to get a viewing when she comes up next week. Her commitment to the peace movement has involved several stints at Greenham Common during the year. EG's contribution to the defence debate was to arrange for Carl-Friedrich von Weizsacker to give the Corbishley Memorial Lecture for the Wyndham Place Trust. This is a most perceptive analysis of East-West relations. It is just being published; if you would like a copy please let us know.

Rachel Heath's death the other day constituted the end of a family friendship extending over forty years and three generations. She had been a friend of both our parents, of most of our generation of the two families, godmother to Becca and Aunt Una to the rest of the children. In the early days at Starvecrow she uncomplainingly coped with them for the weekly bath; Martin was christened in the Chantry; and our move into Lower Belgrave Street was blessed with a liturgy of her devising. RIP.

Undoubtedly the highlight of R's year has been her visit to India from December - February. She writes:

> My reason for going to India was to visit Philip and to learn more about the work of Boys Town Trust whose founder, Joe Homan, I had met in Brussels about 4 years ago through my Belgian friends. The Allards, Antoine and Eleanor, were at that time presidents of Oxfam Belgique and staunch supporters if the Boys Towns. While I was there I became aware of many things besides and the visit has been an experience of rich diversity and many impressions.

Philip joined Joe in Thirumangalam Boys Town, outside Madurai City which boasts of having one of the largest Hindu temples in India, three years ago next February. He has been involved in the training and administration of the BTs which have about 50-60 boys each. There are 7 in S. India now and one and half in Sri Lanka. The boys come from the poor villages of the neighbourhood. Often they are orphans, or their parents cannot feed them or there is illness in the family. Those who are of school age go to the local village schools. Those who have left school at 15 spend the next three years on the farm and are trained in diverse skills depending on what each farm does: animal husbandry, coconuts, coffee and organs, rice, millet, sugar cane, flowers, tomatoes and chili's. In order to meet the demands of the market farmers have to be willing to adapt and change crops; and this happens from time to time. If the monsoons were reliable and if the country could afford modern technology to tap its underground water, southern India (and I presume other parts as well) would be a country of milk and honey. When there is enough rain and where there are enough wells the land can yield three crops a year.

On the back of Phil's motorbike I visited not only the Boys Towns but also his Indian friends who invited us for meals laid out on banana leaves and eaten with the right hand. I learned to enjoy Indian cooking and table-manners. For a week over New Year we travelled by long-distance bus to Ootacamund, a former hill-station with many boarding-schools and churches, to stay with the Bagris. Durga is a radio astronomer who spent about 6 weeks in Cranmer Road with Vimala and Anil their little son when he did a stint at Jodrell Bank some years ago. I was fascinated to see the very different Indian radio telescope and became aware of how much radio astronomers are orientated towards the other planets and the constant rotation of the earth.

Vimala, Anil and we had some good laughs and walks together. English is their language of communication within the family and at work. At the end of the New Year party which they gave for us we and their friends and colleagues who have all worked and lived abroad sang Auld Lang Syne. Being Hindus they do not drink alcohol, so Phil felt somewhat deprived.

In January the RC Carmelite monastery at Cochin, Kerala, held their 2nd Interreligious Seminar. Marcus Braybrook of the World Congress of Faiths in London had drawn my attention to it. So I wrote to Father Albert Nambiaparambil who invited me to come. Going to Cochin involved a long journey by express bus and night train. I went on my own and discovered how easy it was and how friendly people are. The fact that India is an English-speaking country (though with its own brand of English) is a great boon. Once you have adjusted to the cultural and climatic differences you feel very much at home. It was at Cochin that I realised that India is and has been pluralistic for centuries, which accounts for the tolerance and openness of Indian society. An interesting American RC, Professor Ewart Cousins from Fordham University, NY and I were the only non-Indian speakers. He is general editor of an international publishing project, scheduled to appear in print in 1984, on World Spirituality: an Encyclopedic History of the Religious Quest. The subject of the seminar was "Religion and Life, Tradition and Modernity. Professor Cousin and Dr Chincholcar a Hindu from Nagpur University presented secularisation and scientific development as positive opportunities for Religion; I gave a historical resume of interfaith activities in the West starting with the Creation of Councils of Christians and Jews in 1942 and leading up to the new developments in religious Education in British and European schools today.

I believe the seminar has been an important milestone in Indian Inter-religious relations. It decided to encourage the formation of local, regional and national councils to consider such problems as religious education in a pluralistic world society and to cooperate in seeking solutions to the social, economic and political problems of their local and national societies.

I also took part in the 33rd Annual Assembly of the South Asian branch of the World Congress of Faiths. Dr Kahir, a devoted member and worker for interfaith relations, organises these annual events. About 35 Hindus, Muslims and Christians from the professions and businesses in Madurai City attended. I was the only woman. I gave my account once more and suggested more active involvement by the group in the educational and social affairs of the city. This was well received by the younger members.

I have come back from India refreshed, stimulated and profoundly thankful for all I was able to see and learn. India is a great country, the world's largest democracy, and one of the few places in the world where people are still free to do what they like within the bounds of normal human encounter and activity. No wonder it exercises such an attraction to many visitors from the West. I am hoping to go again.

The 1984 letter

THIS WAS THE first year of the European Institute for the Media, which was founded with the help of the European Cultural Foundation in Amsterdam. This attempt to engage in cooperation the media systems of the European Community was much appreciated at the time. Again, our attempts to remove the obstacles to programme production one country being shown in another had borne fruit almost thirty years later. Currently the BBC enjoys showing Danish and Swedish programmes during peak hours in a way that was thought impossible in the 1980s.

18 Cranmer Road
Manchester
M20 0AW

Advent 1984

It seems that this year everyone will be at home for Christmas. For Philip in particular that has become a rarity: but this time he is not due to fly back to Tamil Nadu until the beginning of January. So we all expect to converge on Christmas Eve, Becca from Brighton and Martin from Reading where he is reading for an MA in Applied Linguistics intended to equip him for greater things in the EFL field. Crispin is already on the spot, dividing his time between music and librarianship.

One has the impression that most people will be quite glad to see the end of 1984 with its somewhat ominous overtones. But one of our recent visitors from France, Jean-Daniel Jurgensen, sent us his book on *Orwell ou la route de 1984,* incidentally the first book on Orwell to be published in France, in which he argues that 'reflechir avec Orwell peut nous aider a preserver notre valeur le plus precieuse et la plus fragile: les droits de l'homme, la dignite de l'etre humain et sa liberte'. So perhaps the year will turn out to have had its redeeming features.

For us it has been a busy year. R's return to the College of Adult Education has brought about a remarkable revival of Comparative Religion studies there. Her own course of World Religions attracted capacity participation and there are now two or three others on offer. Instead of one term she seems to be teaching throughout the year.

Her class is made up of an interesting mixture of committed Christians from different denominational backgrounds and one orthodox Jew on the one hand, and non-religious Jews (two of which have no knowledge of Judaism but are politically engaged on the left of the Labour party) and non-church-going Christians like herself on the other. One of the really nice things is to see the orthodox Jew and the Seventh Day Adventist West Indian argue during the coffee break without falling out. They sit together still and in many respects speak the same language.

The College is one of the few purpose-built institutions in the country and enjoys and deserves a good reputation. Its courses cover a wide range and there are 5000 students. R tries to present her course each time under a different aspect, and in this way goes on learning herself. This last term they looked at the ancient religions of the Near East to see anew, or for the first time, the contributions made to Judaism and Christianity by Mesepotamia, Egypt, Canaan, Persia and Greece. The political and social results of their respective imperial activities and achievements were inevitably accompanied by cross-fertilisation and diffusion of religious ideas and practices. Some of the class felt at first that this treatment was undermining their faith. The woman who said this in the beginning gave a short paper at the end showing that this was not so after all. Knowing more about other religions can lead to a greater understanding of one's own.

Since not much has been said in these letters before about the European Institute for the Media, you may like to know how it is developing. The Institute was founded as one of a small group of Institutes linked with the European Cultural Foundation in Amsterdam. The Foundation itself has been active for over a quarter century in the encouraging of European cooperation in education, environmental studies, social policy and political cooperation. Their wish to take an initiative in the media found an echo in the University here where Mark Richmond, the new vice-chancellor and others, were keen to have the Institute.

So EG found himself two years ago with a table and a chair and the job, notionally part-time, to build the new Institute. In the meantime the latter is up to its ears in work: over a dozen research projects concerned with the future of communication in Europe; half a dozen or more seminars and colloquia and a growing stable of publications. The full-time staff consists of a French lawyer, a German sociologist, a New Zealand colleague from the BBC and EG, as well as four support staff of whom two are linguists. There are about ten visiting fellows from five countries who all contribute to specific projects. The working languages are French and English; German may be added if and when the German government can find the money.

One project, to put some flesh on these bare bones, concerns the removal of the obstacles to programmes produced in one European country being shewn in another. Particularly the smaller countries find it difficult to get the UK, France and Germany - let alone the USA - to buy theirs. So they all become excessively dependant on Hollywood castoffs. The Institute is exploring ways of giving Dutch, Danish, Swiss, Portuguese and similar programmes a wider showing. In the course of this the first comprehensive figures about programme flow in Europe have been assembled.

But enough of that. In the summer R and EG were joined at Vigneau by Irmtraut and Klaus-Gunther Gärtner. The house had been occupied during the winter (and is again) by the Escassefort-based Association pour l'Education et l'Insertion des Handicapés. They use the *chais* for movement and musical activities for young people and the Palmiers half to house Patrick de Jenlis who is developing small-scale local industries in which handicapped youngsters can be employed. We are particularly glad to be linked with this initiative and to be able to encourage its support by the unit for the handicapped in the European Commission.

The 1985 letter

W E APPARENTLY DECIDED to attach a copy of the Media Bulletin, published by EIM, to this 1985 Christmas letter. Alas, the Media Bulletin is no long extant. This year also Janet and Martin were married in order to take up Martin's British Council position in Beijing.

18 Cranmer Road
Manchester
M20 0AW

Advent 1985

The neat typeface of this letter comes to you by courtesy of Martin who left us his splendid electronic typewriter when he went to take up a lectureship in English Linguistics at Guangzhou (Canton) University in September. The machine is marvellous but unnerving: from time to time it takes off on its own and can be recalled to base only with difficulty.

Having all been together last Christmas we are about as dispersed as we have ever been this year. Rosemarie, having started off her course on Japanese and Chinese history and religions at the College of Adult Education, has taken the second half of the term off to stay with Philip at Tirumangalam and give some lectures at the Hindu University at Katol in the rural heart of India. Philip had intended to give up his work with the boys Towns Trust at the end of the year. Unfortunately the Trust has not been able to find a suitable successor yet, so that Phil has agreed to stay on for two or three more months. So Rosemarie will stay in India until just after Christmas, returning in time for us to spend a few days over the New Year with Crispin, who is spending some months at Husemann Klinik (7801 Buchenbach near Freiburg) in the Black Forest. The hospital is said to be the best of the Rudolf Steiner-oriented treatment centres anywhere. They are looking into Crispin's medication and giving him a range of occupational therapies. After what was evidently too cerebral a time for him in the early part of the year this period of low-key treatment is doing him a lot of good. He expects to leave there early in the New Year.

Becca has been working at the Brighton Polytechnic most of the year on an interesting assignment aimed at improving the accessibility of its buildings to physically handicapped students. Her work reminds EG of the ergonomic development work on school furniture pioneered in the Architects' and Building Branch of the old Ministry of Education in his time. She has to complete her report by the end of January, and has been wondering whether to develop this typo of work on her own when this assignment ends. Besides this her journal *Mothertongue* seems to be making headway. She is discovering what a lot of work goes into even a quarterly. Although it is run by a cooperative of four girls R and EG can't help feeling that Becca acts as long stop at times of crisis, and that her house (107 Queen's Park Road, Brighton) is effectively the editorial office.

Janet and Martin had been sharing their lives for so long that their marriage in August but set the seal on their union and delighted the more conformist members of both families. They had met, appropriately enough, in EG's old Department in the University, when they were both doing the advanced diploma in TEFL. Then Janet went on to join the staff of the Department while Martin went to Saudi Arabia etc. Now they are both in Guangzhou and have just moved into a flat on the campus of the Foreign Language Institute. Anyone moved to contact them is advised to put Peoples' Republic of China on the envelope. Martin has only five contact hours a week but says that his students are so demanding that at present he spends ten hours on each lecture.

R's lectures have also required new reading. She writes:

Kosuke Koyama's book *Mount Fuji and Mount Sinai* (SCM Press) is an impressive example of religious cross fertilisation and pluralism in Japan. It is also instructive and moving as an account of the spiritual and psychological consequences for the Japanese of their willingness to admit the political presence and economic power of the West about 130 years ago, a response quite different from that of the Chinese who resisted western encroachment. Koyama comes from a Christian family but has retained a perceptive love of his native culture as it has been shaped by Shintoism and Buddhism. What Wesley Ariaraya can only hint at in his postscript to Lesslie Newbigin's *The other side of 1984* (WCC) Koyama expresses profoundly after years of reflection. Chinese history and religions are, if possible, even more fascinating. Besides standard textbooks on Confucianism, Taoism and Chinese Buddhism I find that Fritjof Capra's *The Tao of Physics* illuminates the feel of Eastern mysticism by relating it to the observations and experience of modern sub-atomic physicists. I think the time has come for the West and the East to meet in mutual acceptance and appreciation.'

There is no space to report on EG's Institute: hence for those likely to be interested a copy of the **Media Bulletin** is enclosed.

The 1986 letter

O UR SHILLY-SHALLYING about the European Community continued. I was asked on BBC Manchester one morning whether the EEC directive on lawn mower noise meant that our sovereignty had gone forever. On the larger canvas, the family flourished outside Europe altogether. Rosemarie spent time in India and in China and became more involved in the influence of feminist theology on Christian dogma. When she predicted that in time Indian Hindu and Christian women would want to contribute to theological developments, her hearers were astonished.

18 Cranmer Road
Manchester
M20 0AW

Second Sunday Advent 1986

As we settle down to send you Christmas greetings the London summit seems to have ended in a measure of agreement. When one thinks of Mrs Thatcher's early efforts in Europe the extent of her domestication to the Community atmosphere is remarkable. The United Kingdom nowadays is neither a newcomer not a stormy petrel; that role is played by the Greeks. Odd echoes of past struggles remain: EG was asked on BBC Manchester the other morning whether the EEC directive on lawn mower noise meant that our sovereignty had gone for ever. But in the end even Lord Denning voted for the ratification of the *acte unique*. So the political climate is better than it has been for some years. However, unless ways can be found at long last to reduce expenditure on agriculture the Community will go bankrupt in 1987. No doubt the United Kingdom will be relieved to hand over this Black Peter to the Belgians on January 1st.

The family's preoccupations are, happily, not entirely circumscribed by the Community. EG and the European Institute work closely with the relevant people in Brussels on such matters as the draft directive on trans-frontier broadcasting. But in general the Institute regards the member countries of the Council of Europe as a more appropriate grouping in terms of European broadcasting.

R's concern with Eastern life and religions takes her outside Europe altogether: this year to China to stay with Martin and Janet and to visit the Tings in Nanking. Her second visit to India at the end of last year took her to the Nagpur region to stay with friends she had made at the All-India Interfaith Conference the year before. Nagpur is Hindu India in the way South India is not, because Muslim and Christian families have been living there alongside their Hindu neighbours for many centuries. The Sonak family, with whom she stayed for ten days, gave up their land when Vinoba Bhafe walked through the country persuading landowners to do so. R was taken to see the village elders, the school and rural development projects run by the Ghandian Association. She learnt to eat with her right hand and to live simply in the Ghandian spirit practised by the Sonaks. She visited Ghandi's and Vinoba Bhave's ashrams and was much struck by the continuing influence of these men on their followers. Her most unexpected experience was a visit and lecture to the Jesuit 'Seminar in Nagpur. They asked her to talk about the impact of feminist theology on Christian dogma. Her fears about the way fifty or so young seminarists would take what she had to say proved groundless. They listened with interest and sympathy even when she predicted that, in time, Indian Hindu and Christian women would want to contribute to theological developments and would bring about essential changes. R also spent a day and night with the Madras Jesuits who have long been pioneering cultural convergence between Hindu culture and Indian Christianity; She found the evening service in their chapel illuminating. The low double lotus altar and the liturgical vessels were reminiscent of Hindu temple worship, but the atmosphere of the service conveyed a sense of fellowship and intimacy which is absent from Hindu worship. Apart from the big festivals and regular pilgrimages Hindus don't take to congregational services: they worship either alone or with the family.

Martin and Janet are both on the staff of Guangzhou University now; Janet has taken over some of the lecturing while Martine spends more time on curriculum development for the new emphasis that is being given to English teaching throughout China. In the summer they both went to Kathmandu, Martin largely overland intersecting from time to time with the route taken by his great-granduncle Albert Tafel in search of the source of the Hoang-Ho. Janet was home for a few weeks while Martin was en route and then joined him by air.

Crispin benefited from his time with the Rudolf Steiner community but felt after five months that it was time to come home. The low-key therapy did him good for a time, but he began to miss his musical and other activities. He is working with Graham Turner, the senior Halle clarinettist as well as with Golda Rose, a very gifted art therapist and painter. He has give a number of concerts since his return, two of them in Spain with the London Musicians. As that distinguished journal the *Costa Blanca News* reported, Jill Day and he gave a 'superb performance of Schubert's *The Shepherd on the Rock* for soprano, clarinet and organ in which the artists achieve perfect balance of tonal blend'.

After six months in Australia on terminal leave Philip came home in October only to find himself called in to help the Boys Towns Trust once again. The complexity of the grants the Trust received from public and private sources calls for careful and conscientious management. Since Philip effectively set up the structures, the Trust have asked him to act as consultant to ensure their sound operation. So he is doing that on a part-time basis from London and Peterborough. He also plans to take a course in construction management in the new year to improve his competence on the building side of his rural development work. He is sharing a house in Stoke Newington with friends.

Becca's *Guide for Handicapped Students* for Brighton Polytechnic is now in the press. She is thinking of developing this kind of ergonomic analysis for other organisations. The Arts Council has recently asked all its grant-aided theatres to make adequate provision for handicapped people; and to help the theatres to do so would occupy Becca for quite some time. It remains to be seen whether they are prepared to pay for such help. In the meantime she has also started to work with the Police Monitoring Unit in London with particular responsibility for the treatment of women. Her quarterly also continues on its way.

The 1987 letter

THIS YEAR ONE of EG's friends contributed to the anonymous Crockford Preface whose contents I don't remember. It seems to have related to the Church of England's relationship with other denominations. This also appears to have gone to sleep in the last twenty-five years. The ecumenical consensus to which the C of E contributed during the post-war generation seems to have died. There are few leaders of the Church that any longer taken an interest in Christian reunion. It may be that this is due to the decline of religious awareness in the country as a whole.

18 Cranmer Road
Manchester
M20 0AW

Third Sunday in Advent 1987

We are much behindhand with our Christmas preparations this year, largely owing to EG's peripatetic autumn, of which more below. As it turns out, this has meant that these greetings are being written after that remarkable Reagan-Gorbatchov meeting in Washington which has moved so much further than earlier efforts in manifesting a universal will for peace on earth. As a Christmas present to us all we think it is splendid, however each one's hopes are qualified with ifs and buts.

It is certainly vastly more relevant to the Christian hope than the most-conceived use of the anonymity of the Crockford preface and its tragic aftermath. From our knowledge of some of the dramatis personae we are sure that the intent was much more trivial than the weighty glosses now being put on it. But the whole lamentable affair seems to us to hold a useful warning: the ecumenical consensus in the Church of England which emerged from the war years and the reconstruction period both in ecclesiological terms and in the area of church-state relations is in danger;. The post-war generation has not had the same existential pressures to concentrate on essentials, and has found its rallying points in ultramontanist fantasies or in fundamentalism. We urgently need to rediscover the Christian frontier rather than the evangelical or the anglo-catholic one.

Our family concerns seem to be pretty stable: most of us are doing much the same as we were last year. Becca had a full year with the Police Monitoring Unit in London. She is just finishing her stint which has taught her a lot about the police and more about those who have problems with the force. She is going down to Vigneau over Christmas to reorganise the house after the departure of the squatters we had there for the best part of a year. In the summer they were still firmly ensconced and up to every trick in the French legal book. Equity seems to be unheard of. Fortunately Martin and Philip were able to take a fairly firm line with them during the holidays, aided by a succession of visitors. EG was very glad of this support since he found the whole business rather nerve-racking and retired to Calpe, where R and Becca and Crispin were already installed.

Martin and Janet were home for the long vacation and then returned to canton for another academic year. Given the turnover of expatriate lecturers, they are by now among the doyens of their department, and the Chinese penchant for hierarchy allows them more scope than before to shape the work intelligently. R's visit to them last year included Wouzhou, Nanjing and Souzhhou as well as Guangzhou. Having visited Russia earlier in the decade R was able to compare the two Communist societies. Russia (at the time) so closed and yet full of repressed vitality and intelligence; China open, cheerful and full of curiosity, making one feel relaxed and welcome. Not once in her travels, with Martin or on her own, was she asked to produce her visa or passport. R spent two weeks with M and J in their roomy but draughty flat to share their interesting life. They keep open house once a week for their students and friends and it was heartwarming to experience the affection and friendship between them. Her visit to KH and Sui May Ting and families revived our links with them when KH was Bishop of the Anglican Council, a post-denominational body comprising all non-RC churches and sects. Since the early eighties the CNCC is trying to create an indigenous Protestant church; this requires imaginative and generous leadership- on the part of all concerned.

The theological seminary in Nanjing has taken off again after having been occupied by red guards during the cultural revolution. The churches in Canada, in particular are helping to restock the library and to provide the other material needs. With the help of a guide provided by KH R went to the lovely canal and garden city of Souzhou, the Bruges of the East. In the past retired court officials created their beautiful garden retreats there and practised the Taoist principle of 'living in harmony with nature'.

A month is, of course, too brief a time to do justice to China's ancient history and culture. Bur R returned with a grasp of the three complementary systems of thought and practice: Taoism which teaches human dependence on nature; Confucianism which teaches the importance of good government and of responsible citizenship (hence the long-established concept of central government and the need to train for this); Buddhism which teaches self-knowledge and self enlightenment. Together with the other two this makes up a rich programme for moral endeavour and striving. All religious bodies are represented on the National Council and work out, with the Communists, how the religious freedom clause in the Communist Manifesto affects them.

So much for China. Back in Europe R has become a founder member of the European Society of Women for Theological Research. She believes that feminist theology has an important part to play in the redefinition of Christian experience in new theological language and symbolism as well as in the restructuring of Christian institutions.

Philip's consultancy with the Boys Towns Trust has taken him back to Tamil Nadu for four months for the monitoring of the projects which the Trust is carrying out, particularly with government and with EEC funds. Like many people working in the area of development aid he is putting his emphasis on long-term improvements in the ecological balance of the regions he works in, particularly afforestation. Next summer the Trust intends to begin work in Africa, and they have asked him to direct that. In the meantime he and his friend Maggie (who worked with him in India but is now learning to be a banker at Coutts') intend to take time off to explore the desert fortresses of Rajasthan in January.

Music continues to dominate Crispin's life. This evening he led the clarinets of the Gorton Philharmonic in their festival concert; a few weeks ago he gave a chamber concert with some friends in aid of Neve Shalom; in the summer he joined the London Musicians for their concerts on the Costa Blanca again. But his state of health permits only so much and has to ration himself. The other evening he was very surprised to have a phone call from his friend Natasha in Leningrad who now may be allowed to visit England for two or three weeks. All of us are wondering whether glasnost will actually extend that far.

The European Institute for the Media is flourishing rather too well for EG's comfort. The demands made on it suggest that some people regard it as part of the establishment. It now finds itself identifying middle axioms which escape the big battalions. The European Television Task Force established at our instigation by the European Cultural Foundation in Amsterdam and ourselves is a case in point. As it tours the capitals of Europe taking evidence from the broadcasting organisations and governments, people expect it to be able to solve problems which derive from much larger causes, such as the trend towards deregulation in many European countries, as well as the unregulated development of transfrontier television by direct broadcast satellite.

As a result there is now keen competition between the EEC and the Council of Europe for first place in the achievement of some form of statutory instrument, and the Institute finds itself in the position of the least ignorant agency in the field. Since the move into the Old Medical School the Institute now has quite reasonable accommodation. From he opening last May the Fellows clubbed together to commission a colourful mural from the Greek wife of one of our German colleagues. The library and documentation centre also have better premises and are well used. The University is keen for us to launch an advanced studies programme, and we are quite willing as long as the necessary resources are provided. For the moment there is little movement on that front.

The European scene generally appears to have succumbed to institutional paralysis. There are a few points of growth, however. Giving evidence to the European Television Task Force three weeks ago Lord Cockfield, the Commissioner responsible for achieving the common market by 1992, told us that he had given instruction to the COREPER not to conclude negotiations with the Council of Europe on the television convention until the EEC directive is passed. That is the type of firm action by the Commission that is needed And at a meeting called by Valerie Giscard d'Estaing in Paris last week Helmuth Schmidt proposed a unified European army to be commanded by a French general. Jim Callaghan who was also there pointed out that the UK might have something to say about that as long as there are 70000 British troops in Germany.

This letter has been far too long. We comfort ourselves with the knowledge that no-one need read any or all of it. It comes as always with out warmest wishes for Christmas for 1988.

21. Godfrieda our lovely Zambian daughter-in-law, 1990.

22. The family grows: Rebecca & Shulamit.

23. Crispin & Rainer Diener making music.

24. *The family grows: Martin and Janet with their venerable Morris Traveller.*

25. *The family grows: Philip and Freda do the washing-up.*

26. The family by the pool at Vigneau.

The 1988 letter

THAT YEAR WE celebrated our fortieth wedding anniversary. This was the last time when all eight of the Wedell and Winckler brothers and sisters of our generation were together. Don Cupitt, the founder of the Sea of Faith Movement to which Rosemarie was much devoted, joined us for discussions on the changes in the view of God and the World in the forty years since our marriage. In the European Institute for the Media, Valerie Giscard d'Estaing chaired a task force on Television in the Year 2000.

18 Cranmer Road
Manchester
M20 0AW

Third Sunday in Advent 1988

This time last year we were grateful for the splendid Christmas present to the world at large provided by the successful Reagan-Gorbatchov meeting in Washington. Twelve months later the spontaneous solidarity manifested over the Armenian earthquake is a measure of how far East-West relations have eased. But there is a long way to go. Natasha, Crispin's friend in Lenigrad, who has been trying to visit us for about a year now, has at long last got her passport and visa and should arrive in January. The paperwork involved has been formidable. And only a few days ago we received a reminder that glasnost does not extend to Rumania. A colleague there is virtually a prisoner in his own country because his work on Stalinism remains on the index.

Like most of our contemporaries we are becoming aware of anniversaries which can justify a celebration. So we had a party to mark forty years of married life at Holly Royde in July. Since a lot of people had some distance to come it seemed best to make a weekend of it. On the Saturday evening Crispin and some friends provided some music, including Schubert's Shepherd on the Rock for which Jill Day came up to sing the soprano part. Very sadly

Patrick McLaughlin, who had promised to do a recitation, was in hospital and died shortly afterwards. Patrick's contagious zest for life and his unbounded catholicity had been a joy to us for well over forty years since he was at St Anne's House in Soho. Not least, he christened Martin in the Chantry in the autumn of 1950.

On the Sunday Don Cupitt opened a series of discussions on the changes in the view of God and the World in the forty years since 1948. His remarkable exposition of the paradigm he is working out of the Western Christian tradition provoked a level of cut-and-thrust not often heard since the Epiphany Philosophers' discussions which Kathleen Bliss (who, alas, was not well enough to travel) used to organise on the Third Programme.

For the family it was a unique occasion since all eight of the Wedell and Winckler brothers and sisters of our generation were there, as well as most of the younger generation and our great-nephews and nieces. Martin and Janet arrived back from Canton just in time; Philip and Maggie had not yet left for Zambia; Crispin was already here and Becca came up from Brighton. Since then Becca has moved into our little family flat in London (94 Eton Place, NW3 'phone 0207-722-0299) and has just been appointed to a part-time job in the Camden Library Service. Besides that she is developing her musical interests. The flat is already proving useful for the peripatetic member of the family who need somewhere to stay when they are in London. R and EG make full use of their senior citizen status which has dramatically cut the cost of rail travel and of all sorts of other amenities. In Paris not long ago their railcards provided all-but-free access to the Musee d'Orsay and the Louvre.

Martin and Janet have moved to jobs in Beijing, Martin to the Linguistics Department of the University and Janet to the Foreign Studies University. This entitles them to two flats, albeit in urban tower blocks rather than the sylvan campus setting they enjoyed in Canton. During the long vacation Martin invested in a home base on the banks of the Ribble upstream of Preston, although it is not clear when they will have time to use it. During their two months' reconnaissance of Zambia Philip and Maggie were looked after with much kindness by Willie and Grace Chokani. Willie is shortly to retire and seems keen on joining the rural development project which Philip has been designing. When all the financial arrangements have been made P and M hope to return early in the New Year had to make a start on land not far from Ndola where employment opportunities are declining due to the running-down of the copper belt.

Early in the year R joined the University of the Third Age in South Manchester. She has a group who meet twice a month to study World Religions.

In February shc, EG and the Hughes spent a fortnight in Egypt, most of it in Luxor, the ancient Thebes. Having been a student of SGF Brandon, a noted Egyptologist and historian of religion, R felt at home in the land of the Pharaohs. The cult of Isis and Osiris, the dying and rising saviour-god continued into the 4th century of the Christian era. Alexandria was one of the great centres of Greco-Roman culture and of early Christianity; and the epistles of John may have been written by an Egyptian Christian belonging to the Christian communities mentioned in the Nag Hammadi codex. Not surprising then that one can pick up echoes from the earliest spiritual past of our civilisation to which the Egyptians gave the belief in the resurrection of the body. We marvelled at the imagination and inventiveness with which they integrated the here-and-now with the after life in painting, sculpture and architecture.

We stayed right on the river bank opposite the Valley of the Kings, and were pleased to see that the Nile has lost none of its majestic flow. It was not difficult to grasp Akhenaton's insistence on the splendour of Aton and his worship, given the glorious sunrises and sunsets mirrored in the waters. We spent most of our time in the stupendous temples at Luxor and the tombs in the Valley of the Kings. We also spent two days in Cairo at the Mena-Oberoi opposite the pyramids. We clambered up the narrow passage to the central burial chamber of the Great Pyramid. The son-et-lumiere performances by the Sphinx and at Luxor were impressive and instructive. The Cairo Museum is a must, though the presentation of the treasures has hardly changed since it first opened. The urban sprawl and the notorious extremes of poverty and wealth made us glad to get back to the peace of Luxor.

The report of the Giscard Task Force on the future of television in Europe was published at a conference in Munich in July. It has had a good press, and its main proposal for the creation of a European Television Forum to take over the crumbling national regulatory structures, is likely to be implemented in 1989. But the political obstacles are formidable.

The 1989 letter

A S A RESULT of the breakdown of the Berlin wall and the breakdown of all Communist systems, we called 1989 an anus mirabilis, and twenty-five years later I can only confirm that. The whole of Europe has changed and while we still have problems with the management of Russia, we are now fortunate to operate in a vastly more flexible political context. 1989 was also marked by the birth of Thomas, Philip's son, and our first grandson.

18 Cranmer Road
Manchester
M20 0AW

Advent Sunday 1989

What an annus mirabilis this has been! We have held our collective breaths, and continue to pray that the astonishing outpouring of good sense, *courage civile* and moderation will be sustained into the difficult months ahead. For us it began with the arrival of Natasha, Crispin's friend of many years' standing from Leningrad. It continued with the rapid opening-up of professional links between the Institute and broadcasters and journalists in Hungary, Poland and the Soviet Union. In May the Institute Council decided to establish an East-West Relations Committee; this met in October with newly appointed members from these countries and plans are now in hand for extending the Institute's activities to all countries which sign the Cultural Convention of the Council of Europe. After Christmas we shall spend a few days in Moscow and in Leningrad for the Orthodox Christmas, to see Natasha's family and to consult with some of our colleagues there about future developments.

Earlier in the year it was China that concerned us, since Rosemarie spent the month of May in Beijing with Martin and Janet. Fortunately she had booked her return for June 6, which turned out to be just after the massacre in Tiananmen Square; With the help of a British Council car she got to the airport and left a few hours later. At that stage Martin and Janet thought they would be able to stay, but two days later all Council and Embassy staff were withdrawn. After a drawn-out summer holiday Martin and Janet decided to go back and mercifully found their flats in good order and their belongings untouched. As the senior lecturer responsible for the Applied Linguistics Research Project. Martin now looks after the UK/China commitments in the two Shanghai universities as well as in Beijing.

The Eton Place flat has proved to be a useful base for the development of Becca's freelance activities. She is now building up a gardening business with help from the national Enterprise Scheme, as well as pursuing a diploma course in Community Arts at the London College of Dance on the old Bedford College site in Regents Park. It often seems a curious collection of activities from the outside, but she is happy and fulfilled, and knows where she is going.

Following their reconnaissance in Zambia at the end of last year Philip and Maggie decided to begin on an integrated rural development scheme. Under the auspices of the International Child Care Trust they set up a local foundation, the Kaloko Trust, in Ndola district and were given a 500 hectare site by the government. They have been working very hard with a group of about twenty trainees to get the basic buildings up before the start of the rainy season. Their main unresolved problem is a reliable water supply. A whole series of borings has not so far produced results. Vernon Thomas' Nephew Matthew joined them in October and they expected a Dutch agriculturist to join them in the New Year. They also have a good group of Zambian trustees. So Philip should be able to get away to deal with the other Intercare projects, most of which are in India and Sri Lanka. David Lamont, the Intercare director, has been back in hospital; another reason for Philip as the deputy director to be more mobile in 1990.

Philip and Maggie's Thomas was born in Zambia on 29 July. Fortunately the Lonrho hospital in Luanshia is well-staffed and equipped, so that there was no undue anxiety about having the baby there. Coping with an infant in a mud-brick rondavel without running water is another matter; but they seem to survive. At least there is no shortage of nursemaids. Maggie and Thomas have just arrived home for Christmas; Philip will follow as soon as his assistants can cope.

Crispin much enjoyed having Natasha to stay twice during the year. N found the vast choice available in the shops the most difficult thing to adjust to. Her English is all but perfect: an extraordinary feat bearing in mind that she had never been to England before. Crispin also did the Performer's Certificate of Trinity College of Music and gave the usual series of concerts here and in Calpe. Now he is brushing up his Russian for the visit in January.

During R's visit to China she and Martin spent some days sailing down the Yangtse river to Nanking, where they stayed with the KH Tings again. Besides their intrinsic interest these journeys provide useful material for the World Religion course she does for the University of the Third Age. In September R and EG flew to the island of Milos for the baptism of Roman Luyken, a new godson. In spite of a lot of quarrying and open cast mining Milos retains some splendid beaches. On the way back we had to call in at Strasbourg and Luxemburg, which gave us an excuse to drive from one to the other through the Vosges with an overnight stop at Metz. The cathedral has a wealth of wonderful glass form the 14th century to Chagall: well worth a detour.

The Institute defies all effort to keep it small. The demands for research and for advanced study are stretching our space and resources to their limits. The issues of broadcasting policy which seemed esoteric in 1983 are now the stuff of political controversy; the broadcasting bill in the UK, the directive in Brussels and the new convention in Strasbourg. The Institute's independent stance is not necessarily popular. People wish it would confine itself to 'academic' research (devoid of policy implications). But that, in a field so important to the quality of life, would be a *trahison des clercs*. So we plod on, carefully but resolutely.

The 1990 letter

FOLLOWING THE OPENING up of Eastern Europe, the links between Manchester and Leningrad, which had existed for many years, became normalised. Crispin and we visited Moscow and Leningrad over the Orthodox Christmas, a possibility which we had never thought realistic. The EIM held its second forum in Warsaw, another indicator of the importance of media reform in Eastern Europe.

18 Cranmer Road
Manchester
M20 0AW

Second Sunday in Advent 1990

The autumn for us has been marked by a curious counterpoint of joy and sorrow, in public and personal concerns. On the personal level we have stood by while Ursula, EG's second sister, suffered and died of inoperable cancer of the pancreas. The specialists confessed that there was nothing they could do, and this was confirmed by our Oncology colleagues in the Medical School. As she lay dying we could not help reflecting that Ursula, like rest of our generation, had her life changed by the politics of the 1930's. But for the intervention of Herr Hitler she might well have matched our father's distinguished career at the Bar. As it turned out, the Bar's loss became the gain of the Leicester Magistrates' Bench, not to mention the Mothers' Union. From the way she led us on, more often than not in lederhosen, up trees, on horseback and wherever adventure beckoned, it seemed improbable that she would ever be a housewife and mother. But Harold and the boys became the foci of her life. RIP. The end of the Hitler era in one life coincided with the end of the Hitler era in Central and Eastern Europe. This struck us as we spent time in Warsaw (EG twice, R once) for the European Television Forum (see below) and in Leipzig (EG alone). It has effectively taken the span of

Ursula's adult life for Poland, East Germany and the other countries to start again from where they left off in the late 1930's. Have these fifty or so years been wholly wasted?

Having Maggie and Thomas home for a while in September was a great joy, since we see comparatively little of his development for most of the year. Philip had to stay in Zambia to hold the fort at the Luansobe settlement, which is growing and diversifying all the time. In addition to the trainees (six women and seventeen men) they now have a school, an under-fives clinic, a tannery and leather work training unit, a retail grocery and a grain mill project. At present the people in the area have to make an 85km round trip to get maize ground into mealie-meal. Since the arrival of two more Land Rovers donated by Shaftesbury School a non-profit making taxi service has been started along the sixty-mile stretch of access road which has no public transport. The water situation is still precarious. By applying a technique he learnt in India, that is digging an open well which has reached a depth of thirteen metres, it is possible to pump out a little water each day. They are also building a series of check-dams across the length of the dambo to retain water from seasonal rainfall. Since the summer the Canadian government and the Finnish development agencies have come in with help; but continuing support from a lot of local church and other groups is still needed.

Martin and Janet were home for the summer holidays. Then Janet began an MA course in Durham in Applied Linguistics (which seems to becoming de rigueur for academics in that discipline) and Martin went back to Beijing to plan the expansion of UK technical assistance for Applied Linguistics research and teaching in the universities of North and East China. He hopes to come home for the spring festival holidays at the end of January. Since Janet's sister was teaching in the University of Kuwait and is married to a Kuwaiti film producer, both she and Martin were involved in their problems over the summer and since. Fortunately they were able to get out, but the fate of their family and house in Kuwait City are unknown.

Crispin, R and EG visited Moscow and Leningrad at Epiphany, over the Orthodox Christmas. It was R's second visit and enabled her to visit the Vedernikovs, Nicolai, Nina and their three daughters and grandsons. They were much more relaxed than during R's visit ten years ago. Yet she felt that the Orthodox Church lives in a world of its own, unrelated to the problems and challenges facing the Russian people. Nicolai was able to celebrate the Christmas liturgy in one of the reopened churches and they sang Vespers before she left; a very moving experience. But will they tackle the tasks put before them by glasnost and perestroika?

In Leningrad we spent time with Natasha's grandmother, parents and 13 year old daughter. The two older generations had been idealistic Communists who had given the best part of their lives to the transformation of Russian society. For them the recent changes have been hard to digest; we felt that the effort required to refocus on new concepts and structures is beyond the strength, of the old generations at least. When Natasha was with us for three months in the summer the psychological gap between those brought up during the Soviet regime and the West became apparent. Crispin's condition did not enable him to help N to close the gap. So Natasha returned home in September.

In February R flew to Bombay to visit her friends in Nagpur and Katol. On arrival she found that Padma, her dear friend with whom she was going to stay, had died two days before. Owing to the Hindu custom which requires that the deceased's family should stay in the place where she had died in order to be near the departed spirit; and that the rites for the dead have to be performed there, R spent the inside of a week with the extended family. This enabled her to join the wedding celebration of a distant relative. During the performance of the marriage rites in the home of the bride, she was stuck by the (merely) supportive role of the Brahmin priest who sat on the floor next to the parents who performed the rites for their new son and daughter.

After ten days in the only women's ashram R joined the Sonaks in their home. It was election time and R had lively arguments with Atul about the relative merits of Rajiv Ghandi (whom he supported) and V P Singh (whom R though the better candidate). The campaign methods and the handling of the results by television were reminiscent of those here. R felt again much admiration for the Indians ability to learn from their 'enemies' and to adapt useful customs from their invaders' centuries of occupation. She was very sorry that VP Singh was unable to maintain his coalition or carry the process of democratisation a stage further by letting the lower castes into the civilisation.

The Community Arts Diploma course at the London College of Dance seems to have done Becca a lot of good. She cam through with flying colours and is now building up her counselling practice. This of course is a slow business, so she continues with some gardening to make ends meet. In September she spent four weeks or so with Georg and Leda Lyken and EG's godson Roman on the island of Milos. Georg has now left the Institute to build up a programme export business in Munich. He was replaced by a Norwegian as head of research in the Institute.

Besides the regular round of chamber concerts Crispin played at a concert in aid of Rumanian orphans in May. In June he went out to Zambia to visit Philip and Maggie at Luansobe, where his playing was also much enjoyed. He now has a more varied group of musicians playing with him. This makes it possible to enlarge the repertoire of the concerts. Once a week he drives to Lancaster to meet a psychotherapist with whom he has developed a good working relationship.

The Institute has reached a point in its development where it should have the resources to grow into a new phase. It has become recognised around Europe (now East, Central and West) as the least worst instrument for the development of a coherent media policy. It is not universally popular because it is beholden to none of the big interests in this field. On the other hand it is valued for the quality of its work, as was indicated by the award of the Belgian Prix Bernheim to Andrew Lange, one of our research workers, for the work he did on our report on the future of the European audiovisual industry; the award of an honorary degree to Sir Frank Roberts, one of our vice-chairmen; and the appointment of EG as a Chevalier of the Ordre des Arts et des Lettres by the French government earlier in the year.

The problem is how to provide the financial infrastructure for the new phase. We have been approached by two or three places in other parts of Europe, which would like to house the Institute and would provide it with more substantial basic finance. These explorations continue, although EG particularly would be very sad not to continue in Manchester. The UK members of the council are exploring whether the government in its post-Thatcher phase is more inclined than before to make some effort to keep it in the country.

In the meantime the second European Television and Film Forum took place in Warsaw in November, and was much better established than the first. Both the participation and the substance were more substantial. The publication of *Freedom and Control*, a vade mecum for politicians and broadcasting administrators in Central and Eastern Europe, as they make their broadcasting systems more democratic, has been much appreciated. The volume is doing the rounds and is likely to be useful for some time.

EG has given notice that he would like to retire from the directorship of the Institute in 1992. He will have done ten years and would like to have a little more time to think and write. If you have any names you can suggest for the succession, please let him know. It is a demanding but fascinating job for someone with senior academic and practical media experience, either in the press or in broadcasting.

The 1991 letter

IN THE ABSENCE of proper support for the EIM in this country, the Institute Council accepted the invitation of the Prime Minster of North Rhine-Westphalia to move the Institute headquarters to Düsseldorf. We tried to keep the EIM's Advanced Studies Unit in Manchester.

18 Cranmer Road
Manchester
M20 0AW

Second Sunday in Advent 1991

Writing this letter on the eve of the Maastricht summit we cannot but reflect that we have been here before. The essential cession of sovereignty took place when we entered the European Community in 1973. Every step taken since then derives from that: EMU, subsidiarity, the democratic deficit, political cooperation, defence et al. On EMU we have been interested in the practical application of this which the Institute has had to do in order to relate salaries and wages here to the scales we have to apply when the headquarters of the Institute move to North Rhine-Westphalia (see below). Middle and upper level salaries in Germany are not very different from here; it is at the bottom that there is a differential of about a third. Thus it is quite true that EMU will cause labour market problems, but these can be dealt with if we can increase productivity at that level. When EG was in Brussels he always worked on the principle that nothing should be done there which could be better done at the local, regional or national level. And, particularly on the social charter (the first draft of which he had a hand in before it was put on the shelf during the 1974 oil crisis), it is reasonable to establish a floor below which no provision should fall. Above that let each member state do what it will.

But enough of that. On the family front there has been much coming and going during the year. Rosemarie was in China again in May; Martin was home in February and in August-September. Janet finished her MA in Applied Linguistics at Durham and went back to Beijing in October. Philip was here en route to and from a tour of International Childrens Trust (ex-Boys Town) projects in Thailand, India and Sri Lanka. Maggie and Thomas were home for August; EG spent a week at Luansobe in June, etc. The Kaloko Trust project there which Philip has built up is now on a more even keel. The UK High Commission having judged it the best project of its kind in Zambia. The UK Overseas Development Administration will now support it to the extent of 50%. At the same time the Boys Towns Trustees finally came to a definitive break with Joe Homan. They changed their personnel and reoriented their work as Philip had suggested. Thus they also have resumed their support of the Luansobe project. We hope that Christian Aid will now also come in. The first 'graduates' of Luansobe have begun to fend for themselves on their 10 hectare plots (rather over 20 acres), and Philip is keeping a close eye on their progress.

The Zambian elections were a cheerful surprise: perhaps the spread effect of pluralist ideas in Eastern Europe will encourage peaceful change in Africa also. Making pluralism work is another matter in which the Institute is much involved. Having distributed widely throughout Central and Eastern Europe a little vade mecum on the creation and management of pluralist broadcasting systems, it has found an insatiable demand for advice, support and training. A colloquium on The Political Content of Broadcasting in Budapest in September brought together politicians and broadcasters from Poland, Czechoslovakia and Hungary with some of their opposite numbers from Western Europe. The effect of this kind of cooperation on the new media laws and practice in these counties is incalculable. EG was invited to serve on the International Advisory Council of the Hungarian Broadcasting Corporation and is due in Budapest again next week.

The invitation from the Prime Minister of NRW to move the Institute to Düsseldorf, his capital, was accepted by the Institute Council last June. The decision followed consideration of approaches from Amsterdam, Barcelona and Strasbourg, as well as energetic efforts to raise the £3-400 000 necessary for the Institute's development here. In the event the state of NRW which is autonomous in matters of cultural and media policy, satisfied the Institute's quadrilateral of conditions mainly concerned with its independence and long-term support. The Advanced Studies Unit will remain in Manchester; the other departments will move to Germany next June. EG will see them through the move and the first few months, and hope to be retiring by the end of 1992. That date also marks the tenth anniversary of the Institute's foundation, and is a good point at which to let a new director-general take the tiller for the next stage of the Institute's development.

During the autumn EG and R have also been adapting the house so as to provide a study at ground floor level for Rosemarie and more elbow room in the kitchen. The re-roofing of Vigneau with non-slip pantiles should make major building work unnecessary once we retire. Vigneau was occupied for most the year by tenants and friends. In September twelve members of the Chantry Group had an old-fashioned reading party there, re-reading Simone Weil's *Waiting on God*, Anthony Storrs' *Churchill's Black Dog* and other Essays and Noel Annan's *Our Age*. By common consent *Waiting on God* seemed to speak to the present day even more than on its publication forty years ago.

Martin and his Chinese colleagues are putting the finishing touches to their new book on the methodology of language teaching. On the whole, though, he seems to be fairly gloomy about the effectiveness of the substantial investment the British Council are putting into the Chinese universities on the language front. The Tiananmen Square trauma persists and has set back the opening up of the Chinese higher education system to new ideas. Both Martin and Janet feel that by the end of the present academic year they will probably have done as much as they can, given the present constraints.

Becca's Music Therapy practice is building up steadily. She has both adult and younger students, and the flat is choc-a-block with all sorts of instruments. Economically the practice is as yet precarious, but Becca is determined to remain independent so as to remain free to develop her own methods. Having urged the young to strike out on their own EG can hardly complain, but a life time spent in the cocoon of (largely) big organisations leaves him nervous about too much freelancing. But the Chalk Farm flat is a useful location for Becca's type of practice. Crispin goes down to stay there with her from time to time when he is not too busy with his various musical activities. He now has two excellent tutors and a splendid accompanist. Their work has much improved Crispin's interpretative capabilities. He now has a soprano saxophone which he is learning to play with Jonathan Rebbek, a member of the excellent Apollo Saxophone Quartet.

In May R was in China again and went with Martin to see the terracotta soldiers in Shian: a very impressive sight. Outside the city the cornfield were going brown from the rain, foreshadowing a bad harvest and the terrible flooding in the Yangtze delta. Fortunately her friends in Nanjing were spared the worst. There Prof Chen Xin booked her into the University guest house. In talks with him and the Tings and other Chinese friends she became aware of the great desire of thinking Chinese for change and glasnost. But their memories of the Cultural Revolution and the current developments in the USSR make them willing to be patient. In fact patience was a word much used. Our contacts with the post-experience students brought over by the British Council show that they go back with a quiet determination to work and wait for change. This is probably the best that can be done for the moment.

In July R attended a **Sea of Faith** conference in Leicester. It was an interesting experience. She made new friends and met Ruth Robinson again. One of the outcomes of the conference is a quarterly meeting in the North, most recently last Saturday near Blackpool. At the conference of the European Society of Women for Theological Research in Bristol in September Ursula King, Professor of Religious Studies, was the host. It was valuable to meet some of the leading feminist theologians: Dorothee Soelle, Rosemary Radford-Ruether and Anne Primavesi among them. Two charming young woman from London, two woman Protestant pastors form Hungary, a dynamic Portuguese MEP and a remarkable Caribbean woman minister were only some of the lively theologians there.

In October there was a short sortie to Malta with EG which whetted her appetite to return with him at leisure; and a week in Germany with her sisters, where they all took part in the bicentenary of the family trust set up by her mother's family. The party included a coach tour in the former GDR. It was a salutary shock to see the ruinous desolation of towns and villages; the task which the two Germanies face together; and the degree of patience and generosity required of them in order to bring about real integration.

R also represented, with three other pilgrims, the Beatrice Hankey Foundation at the opening of new buildings for Lagan College, the first integrated secondary school in Northern Ireland (which the Foundation has aided). Although NI is a sad region with an isolated and divided society, the past ten years have seen the growth of the school from 28 to 750 pupils, supported by both protestant and catholic parents, teachers and children. It is also supported by innumerable people throughout this country, Europe and the USA, some of whom took part in the happy celebrations. So there is hope: hope in things not yet seen holds the world together and will bring it to ever-closer unity in the future. R feels very thankful for the blessings in her and the family's life in 1991.

The 1992 letter

THE EIM AT this time was much in demand to oversee the democratisation of the television systems in the former Communist states. I was much involved in this trend and I see the 1992 letter was begun en route between Novisad in Serbia and Szeged in Hungary, continued at the airport in Budapest, and finished in the Institute's comfortable headquarters in Düsseldorf. While I was engaged in those matters, Philip developed his training for farmers in Zambia. So the family was much engaged in European and world-wide matters. My successor was appointed. The German members of the Institute Council wanted a German to succeed me, and succeeded in finding Bernd-Peter Lange, a Professor in Osnabrück.

18 Cranmer Road
Manchester
M20 0AW

Third Sunday in Advent 1992

Our Christmas greetings this year have had to be written in the interstices of a particularly mobile Advent season. Although R has been able to write her contribution in Manchester, EG has had to go to Belgrade, as well as commuting between Manchester and Düsseldorf during the time when we would normally expect to have a weekend clear.

The letter was begun en route between Novi Sad in Serbia and Szeged in Hungary while waiting for passport clearance at the frontier. It was continued in the airport at Budapest, and is now about to be completed in the Institute's comfortable headquarters in Düsseldorf.

On re-reading last year's letter, Maastricht was already a live issue and EG wrote "When George Wedell was in Brussels, he always worked on the principle that nothing should be done there which could be better done at the local, regional or national level". So much for the Old Moore's role of the

Christmas letter!

R's most important experience during the year was her visit in May to the Kaloko Trust settlement in the Luansobe Forest, ninety kilometres south of Ndola in the Zambian Copperbelt. There Philip, his trainees and workers have created a new village and farming community with a school and boarding houses, a shop, a dairy and a piggery, a brick and tile making unit, a mechanic's workshop, dormitories and rondavels for the trainees, staff and guests, as well as a full-scale farming operation.

The main problem at Luansobe has always been the lack of water. But by now the huge tank, which in May was still being dug even deeper down to the water table, will have been filled by the rains which have arrived at last. By means of strict rationing throughout the year the settlement has water for cooking, washing and selective watering. Now there will be celebrations as the tank fills up and becomes a reservoir.

It was a great pleasure to be with the young men and women who spend two years on the training course. They have names like Wisdom and Lovemore, as well as the more conventional Jackie, Alex and Jessie. They learn to do all jobs themselves. I shall never forget coming across Jackie, a beautiful Zambian woman, under a tractor doing repairs. Who would heave expected to see that in the middle of nowhere? The community have a cheerful and positive attitude to their work. The first group of trainees are now building their own community on 25 acre plots for each young farmer about 35 kilometres from Luansobe. They set out on a cooperative basis to become viable market gardeners with some stock rearing.

R had welcome and farewell parties. Wisdom very ably delivered the speeches each time. For the farewell the schoolchildren and staff, trainees, workers and their families gathered round a huge bonfire to spit-roast a suckling pig. The school children sang, the Kaloko band played and everyone danced. It was a truly happy occasion and R felt much honoured to be proclaimed "mother of Kaloko" in a speech.

At preset Martin and Janet are at Luansobe at the end of their sabbatical after six years in China. Martin spent part of the year at the University of Southern California in Santa Cruz doing a course in Agro-ecological farming. Much as he enjoyed it, he came to the conclusion that he is too much of an academic to make a habit of it. Nonetheless he looked after the kitchen garden at Luansobe; and Crispin has to sent out exotic seeds from time to time. Janet will be going out to Hungary for the British Council in the New Year and Martin intends to follow a little later.

Philip was home in the summer and brought with him a tape about

Luansobe made by a South African film crew. If any of you want to borrow it, pleas let us know. Maggie unfortunately could not stand the pace, and has come home to her base in Eastbourne with Thomas. They spent part of the holiday at Calpe with us, where Tom had his first experience of sea and sand. He now goes to a nursery school while Maggie trains to qualify as a physiotherapist.

In November R and EG went on a brief visit to Israel, where EG had to open a new Media Faculty in the Business School. They were glad to see the country again after thirteen years, especially since they were able to meet Israelis at work and in their homes. Most of those they met are anxious for the government to bring about more radical changes more quickly, and to tackle the Palestinian problem more vigorously. R particularly enjoyed lunch at Neve Shalom-Wahat at Salaam, the Israeli-Palestinian Community and School for Peace perched on a hillside near the Latrun Monastery between Jerusalem and Tel Aviv. Crispin and his friends have given an annual concert for them ever since R met Father Bruno, their founder. Coral Aron, who with her late husband Wellesley, helped to establish the School, showed us round. There are strong similarities between the Northern Irish and Israeli situations. Lagan College in Belfast is the first integrated secondary school in the Province; Neve Shalom is a pioneer in Israel. Both have now been recognised by their respective Ministries of Education; but at Neve Shalom the need for funds remains as great as ever. We left determined to carry on with our small contribution to this eminently worthwhile enterprise.

Becca completed the Community Arts Diploma at Goldsmiths' College last summer, and is not, as far as one knows, at present doing anything academic. Her practice continues to develop, particularly on the geriatric side. How pioneering this work is we cannot say, but she much enjoys it and seems to be in growing demand. She hopes to dispose of her share of the Brighton house in the near future. Crispin and she contributed to the musical side of the Chantry Group meeting at S. Katherine's in November.

EG's successor has now been appointed. He is Bernd-Peter Lange, Professor of Economic Theory in the University of Osnabrück, who has been involved in the policy-making side of the media in the Federal Republic. He was chosen from about fifty candidates from all over Europe. So EG will retire on 31 March next. That will be a blessing since he finds the regular commuting much more exhausting than when he first went to Brussels twenty years ago.

It is nice to be able to hand over a going concern so well housed and staffed. In the meantime work goes on apace. Having been asked by the

British presidency of the Council of Ministers to monitor the access to the media of the candidates in the Romanian general election in September, the Institute is now doing a similar job for the Serbia and Montenegrin elections on December 20th. Hence the tortuous journey to Belgrade, cut off as the city is by sanctions.

The welling-up of age old animosities between the successor states of Yugoslavia is due largely to the Croats and the Serbs, although the latter blame the Germans for forcing through the premature recognition of Croatia. Since I learned all about the Sanjak of Novibazar in the fifth form I never thought I would have to bother about it again. But here it is: one of the possible flash points between Orthodox Serbs and Muslims on the historic borderline between the Ottoman Empire and the Hapsburg dominions. The Institute's monitoring team is not very sanguine about these elections being either fair or free.

The range of Crispin's musical activities has expanded during the year. He does a fair number of engagements nowadays. In addition he has decided to do the performer's Diploma of Trinity College of Music. Now that retirement beckons for EG we have lots of plans for exploration of those parts of Europe which have been closed to us for so long. Crispin's undoubted skills as a map reader and navigator will be very useful. It will be interesting to pursue the Danube to the Black Sea; having crossed it twice in the last week, it seem to provide one of the major remaining wetlands in Europe.

The 1993 letter

IN 1993, Rosemarie continued her work in India. The Media Institute celebrated its tenth anniversary with a dinner in the House of Commons and a colloquium in the BBC Council Chamber under the stern gaze of John Reith. Sir Karl Popper contributed a sombre analysis of the relationship between civilisation and the control of violence.

18 Cranmer Road
Manchester
M20 0AW

Second Sunday in Advent 1993

This Advent tide the world remains a nervous place, though not necessarily the worse for that. The two major advances we think, have been the outbreak of cooperation in South Africa and the beginnings of a rapprochement in the Holy Land. The possibility that the contagious effect of these events may lead to peace in Northern Ireland waxes and wanes as this letter is being written. We find it depressing that progress is often so slow. The people who live in all these countries and in East and Central Europe are tempted to think they knew where they were under the old regimes, and to wonder whether the upheavals which accompany liberalisation are worthwhile. When pressed, most people are quite clear that they do not want to go back to the old regimes. The world is now a more open place; and there are few countries without an open society left. And that is a blessing we must surely give thanks for.

Rosemarie was in Zambia again in April - May for three weeks. It is remarkable how the training scheme and farm settlement at Luansobe have developed into a village-community with its school, a health clinic nearing completion, and now also a community and adult-education project. Rosemarie was able to discuss the latter with some of "the leading lights" while she was there and is thrilled to read how they are working on it. She is hoping to see for herself when she goes again in the spring of 1994.

In August - September Rosemarie spent a month in India, participating in Bangalore, South India, in the centenary celebrations of the first World Parliament of Religions in Chicago in 1893. India's Vivekananda and other philosophers at the time were responsible for getting the Interfaith Movement launched. It was fitting therefore, that three of the major celebrations should take place in India. Since Rosemarie had taken part in the British Centenary Festival in London last January she did not go to the Centenary Retreat at Kanykumari, right at the tip of India, nor did she go on to Delhi, Chicago and Tokyo like some of her fellow-conference members.

In Bangalore Rosemarie opted for a programme of visits. Every day her group visited selected religious communities in and around Bangalore, where they experienced different religious emphases and practices as well as generous hospitality. There were official receptions given by the state government of Karnataka and ministers came to speak at some of the plenary sessions.

After the official end of the conference Rosemarie stayed another two days at Bangalore visiting the branch-Ashram of the sisters of the Paunar Ashram in Maharashtra. Then she took the weekly Bangalore-Delhi train, alighting 24 hours later at Nagpur. The remaining three weeks she spent visiting her Indian families at Katol, Aurangabad and Bombay. Fortunately none of the families live near the epicentre of November's terrible earthquake in the state of Maharashtra. She had a most enjoyable and refreshing as well as politically interesting time, since India was still smarting from the violent demonstrations and massacres carried out by Hindu and Muslim communities. She had interesting discussions with her Hindu friends about the desirability or otherwise of the apparent strength of the BJP party. According to the latest news from India it is losing its grip now. Some of her friends were more in favour of its aims, not its methods, than others. Her Muslim friends in Katol continued to feel secure in their position in the local community.

With their Hindu friends in this small country town in the Nagpur District where they had not experienced the communal upheavals in other parts of India. She returned in September mentally refreshed even if physically reduced by a stone, to her family and household commitments, with her love for her Indian friends and for Indian democracy strengthened and deepened. Now she is hoping that one or two Indian friends will come to Manchester in a year or two.

In October/November we enjoyed the visit of Inge Ghosh, an old Wistow-sister now living in Canada, who divided her time between Manchester, Belfast and Sevenoaks. With her we share many remembered and forgotten experiences during the years 1943-1946.

Martin and Janet are, as we thought last year, well established in Hungary as part of the British Council team which is modernising the teaching of English. Martin is deputy director of the centre for English Teacher Training in the University of Debrecen, the centre of Hungarian Calvinism; and Janet does a similar job at a teacher training college nearby. For us it is good to have them relatively, i.e. only one time zone away. In that way we can see more of them. They, for their part, become much engaged with the efforts of the Hungarians to rejoin the European comity of nations, in spite of the rearguard actions of some neo-Stalinists and nationalists to prevent this.

We spoke too soon last year about Becca's completion of academic work. She has now decided to do a degree in music, and is struggling with the preliminaries for this alongside her work. This seems to be flourishing, and she is in substantial demand for remedial musical activities. The flat is coming to be too small for all her teaching activities. But anything larger will have to wait until she disposes of her share of the Brighton house. Having for many years regarded opera as a bourgeois interest, she has now discovered its universal appeal, and spends time in the gods at Covent Garden.

Martin and Crispin are off later this month to spend the Christmas holidays at Luansobe with Philip. Martin justifies this by the need to see how 'his' kitchen garden and experimental plots are getting on; Crispin by taking out treble recorders to see whether the children at the primary school can be taught to make use of them. Crispin is steadily occupied as usual by a series of musical activities. He has re-started work on harmony and composition with Roger Wilkes, the former Head of Music at the College of Adult Education, which is one of the many victims of Thatcherism in this city. It is now an annexe of our newly-named Metropolitan University of Manchester, the fourth university level institution here.

The work of the Kaloko Trust at Luansobe continues to grow. In September William and Grace Chokani were here for a night (Willy is the chairman of the Trust), and talked about the extension of the Luansobe principles to other countries in Southern Africa. Willy, who was Minister of Labour in the first Malawian government after independence, is now going back to help to rebuild democratic institutions there. Evidently the Young Pioneers of the Banda era are being used to prevent this.

Philip was home for more than two months earlier in the year to deal with Kaloko matters, and to sort out the arrangements for Thomas and Maggie. That having been done, Tom went out to Zambia with Phil for a month before starting schooling in Eastbourne in September. The rainy season seems to

27. Grandma and Tom painting Easter eggs, 1994.

28. Grandpa and Emily in Vigneau, 2008.

29. Rebekka with her daughter Chanya in Ireland, 2005.

30. Tom & Emily at their grandparents Diamond Wedding Anniversary, 2008.

31. Chanya & Lina in Hungary, 2011.

32. Emily, Chanya and Isaac, 2008.

33. Uncle Martin and Tom playing rough and tumble, 1992.

Vernon Thomas with Tom and Maggie at Luansobe, 1989.

Philip and Tom at Luansobe, 1990.

have been satisfactory; the reservoir is full and the harvests have been good.

The Media Institute celebrated its tenth anniversary in June with a dinner in the House of Commons and a colloquium in the BBC council chamber under the stern gaze of John Reith. It was a good occasion, and EG came in for a good deal of reflected glory, including yet another decoration, this time from the President of Portugal. Tony Pragnell edited a commemorative volume *Opening-up the Media 1983-93*, whose twenty or so contributors demonstrated how the media landscape in Europe has changed out of all recognition. Sir Karl Popper contributed (by videotape) a sombre analysis of the relation between civilisation and the control of violence; this is a theme which I hope the Institute will now take up, possibly in cooperation with the Annenberg Washington Programme.

The 1994 letter

IN 1994, WE BUILT THE SWIMMING POOL at Vigneau. It became important for us and for our guests, to whom it proved a great boon. At the end of May I was asked to give away the prizes on Speech day at my old school, Cranbook. Since my time, the school has become the only secondary school in the Weald of Kent. It has become co-educational; the boys and girls come from a splendid mix of backgrounds: local, national and worldwide. I can't think why the Cranbook model, which goes back to the first Queen Elizabeth, has not been developed more actively to integrate public schools and the national education system.

18 Cranmer Road
Manchester
M20 0AW

Second Sunday in Advent 1994

This year has been the first full year of retirement, and our pace and mode of life have changed a good deal for the better. No longer the 6.30 starts for the airport on Mondays; no longer the weekends catching up with the post. For EG certainly, the pace has become much more leisurely as he spends a lot more time at Cranmer Road. Rosemarie and Crispin have on the whole coped with this change very well; even the adage about R's having married EG "for life but not for lunch" has gone out of the window.

Our guest room has been turned into an office with computer, printer, fax and photocopier, as well as an elaborate telephone system. Pauline, the secretary comes one and half days each week; other aides and researchers turn up regularly. So when EG is at home the house hums like a beehive. It is a good thing that Crispin has the attic and I have the studio to retire to. Fortunately, I am still teaching my class for the University of the Third Age fortnightly, and am a member of the North-West network group of Sea of

Faith, and have good friends. We also enjoy going to the theatre, ballet, opera and have Halle and Royal Northern College of Music season tickets. We go either a deux, as a trio or with friends. There is never a dull moment and much to be thankful for.

So we have been spared the traumas of retirement. To those, and there were many, who asked "what on earth will you do?" the answer is that EG now does only what he can cope with comfortably. That is a great relief after 46 years as a wage slave at other people's beck and call. However enjoyable working life was, and a good deal of it was very enjoyable, it has been splendid to bid farewell to the pressures. For the moment there is still more than enough work to do.

One of the joys is that R and EG can go off together more than in the past. In June-July we had a leisurely time at Vigneau. Among other events we commissioned the new swimming pool, which has already proved a great boon to all ages. Philip's Thomas was the youngest swimmer and Mabel Wilkins, (at ninety the oldest) insisted on a daily swim before breakfast, rain or shine. The heat exchanger produces a comfortable 28 degrees or more; so not much moral fibre is needed to dive in. In September we had the second Vigneau Reading Party. We compared Dietrich Bonhoeffer's **Letters and Papers from Prison** after fifty years, with Don Cupitt's **After All; Religion without Alienation** (SCM Press 1993); and read Dorothy Emmet's **The Role of the Unrealisable** (Macmillan 1993); and did a part-reading of Tom Stoppard's **Arcadia**.

At the end of May EG gave away the prizes at Cranbrook, his old school. The invitation coincided with the 50th anniversary of his leaving. Cranbrook is now co-ed and, as a grant-maintained school, enjoys many of the advantages of independence while leaning heavily on public funds. The boys and girls come from a splendid mix of backgrounds, local, national and worldwide: I can't think why the Cranbrook model which goes back to 1574 has not been developed a more actively for integrating public schools into the national system.

In July we were invited by the Dean of Chichester to attend a service to mark the 50th anniversary of the 1944 attempt to kill Hitler and restore legitimate government in Germany, and the roles which George Bell and Dietrich Bonhoeffer played in that tragic endeavour. George Carey preached a well thought-out sermon.

We thought the effort worthwhile since memories are so short. For a lot of the congregation that period is by now only a matter of hearsay. It was a lovely day and over a sandwich lunch in the Dean's garden we met a lot of old friends, not least Edward and Ellen Gumbel whom we had not seen for 40 years or so.

Last New Year Klaus Meyer suggested that we should travel the Silk Road together. So in late March we set out for Uzbekistan. On arrival in Samarkand we landed in the ice box of the local Intourist hotel. The central heating had been turned off on March 15th, the hot water boiler was only partially working. At least we had brought our hot water bottles which were filled by our floor babushka.

The splendid architecture of Registan Square with its mosque and madrasa seminaries, the superb mosaics which decorate the in - and outside of the buildings in glorious colours and patterns, made up for the discomfort in the hotel. So did our visits to other historic and artistic monuments like Tamerlaine's mausoleum and mosque, and our interesting outing to the mountains on the road to Afghanistan. Uzbekistan was the central section of the Silk Road from China in the East to the Mediterranean world in the West. The Silk Road represented the first intercontinental trading system in history. Its importance ceased when the Portuguese sailed round the Cape and into the South China Sea. The sense of history is overwhelming: the Persians incorporated the region into their empire, hence their interest in it now. They were succeeded by Alexander who occupied and held it en-route to India and back. Then it was taken over by the Arab Muslims who introduced their faith. The Mongols overwhelmed it in the 12th century and established their Pax Mongolia throughout their vast conquered territories for a while. Lastly Tamerlaine, a local aristocrat, took over until his descendants were replaced by local Emirs and their tribes who ruled the area up to the 19th century. Russia defeated Britain in the 'great game' and, after the Russian revolution the whole of Central Asia was incorporated into the Soviet Union.

Bukhara too has splendid mosques and madrasas, most of them being slowly repaired and restored. The Sufis and the Dervishes had their centres and monasteries there. The main building with its terrible reputation, is the Ark or Citadel in the centre from where the Emir carried out his brutal control. We were taken to see the special dungeon, the bug-put, where among many others two British officers/diplomats were kept for years only to be executed in the end. I hope I have succeeded in whetting your appetite for a visit to this historically fascinating part of Central Asia.

A three-day detour to Delhi (where we had our first really hot baths) gained in significance when our express train from Delhi deposited us at the splendid palaces, mausoleums and cities of the Mogul emperors of India, Agra and Fatahput Sikri. The Taj Mahal in particular is one of the exquisite wonders of the world. It was Babur, the great-grandson of Tamerlaine who founded the Mogul empire and between him and his successors created the unique blend of Islamic/Hindu architecture there: wonderful.

In February EG was in Hungary again for a meeting organised by the opponents of the then regime. It was at a time when the Government was preparing for the next elections in April, and was intent on preventing the oppositions from gaining a fair hearing on the radio and television. So a large number of dissident journalists were dismissed from the media organisations. But this did not prevent the ruling party from being defeated and replaced by a coalition of the Socialists and Liberal Democrats. Martin and Janet observed all this from their perch in Debrecen. We spent an enjoyable weekend in the historical Gellert hotel in Budapest. Since Martin was still suffering some of the ill-effects of his African trip we could not, alas, make as much use of the thermal baths as we had hoped. Janet did not enjoy her year in the outback of Hungary near the Ukranian border. So she opted to return to Beijing where the British Council had a job for her. For the moment they are commuting between Debrecen and Beijing, which is not the most convenient arrangement.

Philip was home twice during the year. So we saw him and Tom relatively frequently. The Kaloko Trust's projects continue to expand. They now cover so wide a range of activities that Philip and his friends have decided to establish a Kaloko (UK) Foundation. This will, of course, cooperate on specific projects, such as the school, with the International Children's Trust and others. But it will ensure that the specifically integrative character of the Kaloko model does not get lost in a multitude of other good causes.

Becca has just started a Bachelor of Music course at Goldsmiths, having passed her music 'A' level with flying colours in the summer. Taking the course alongside her job will make it a long and arduous haul. Crispin started in the autumn to work in the Hallé orchestra library twice a week. This brings him into contact with the mechanics of running an orchestra. He seems to get on well with Patrick Williams, the librarian.

One of the jobs which has taken quite a lot of EG's time has been the assembly with Renate, and writing, of a memoir of their parents. The Church of the Rhineland are to publish this. Gertrude's autobiographical sketches written in the 1950s form the centre-piece. Two chapters about the earlier years and another two about the years after 1950 had to be written. Since Hans were born in 1881 and Gertrude died in 1979 they managed between them to all but cover a momentous century. The book is now in the press. We hope the volume will make a modest but interesting contribution to the history of our times.

In the early summer the Leverhulme Trust gave EG one of their Emeritus Fellowships for retired Professors who have not finished all that they should have done while they were working. The Fellowships provided help with research, travel and secretarial expenses. Wit this EG hopes to produce a volume on **The Public Interest in Broadcasting**. At the same time, a project concerning the relationship between television and democracy in Africa came to fruition. With his colleague Jean André Tudesq, who is the Director of the Communications Institute in Bordeau, he intends to look at the situation in the Ivory Coast, in Kenya and in Mozambique. Olivia Henley will be the research associate; her knowledge of Portuguese will enable the team to deal with Mozambique.

The 1995 letter

IT WAS A good year for the Liberal Democrats in Manchester; they began to move into a position where they could form the majority on the Council. I encouraged them to think about what they would do about education.

18 Cranmer Road
Manchester
M20 0AW

Second Sunday in Advent 1995

This has been a year of jubilees. The 50th anniversaries of the end of the war in Europe and in the Far East, as well as of the dropping of the first H-bomb, concentrated our minds on both the importance and the cost of peace. There were also a spate of golden weddings, proving that the majority of people remain, as before, committed to life-long marriage. Roger and Patricia Gillett celebrated in steady rain in their splendid marquee in Altrincham. Michael and Christl Lethbridge's was in a village hall near Guildford and included some splendid musical performances. We could not get to Bob and Peggy Stones' at the Overseas League, but managed to catch the end of Bob's one-man show at the 47 Gallery.

Talking about paintings, EG wanted to have Rosemarie's portrait done for her birthday. In the end she agreed, provided it was a joint portrait. After some enquiries with the Royal Society of Portrait painters we hit on Trevor Stubley, their Vice-President, who lives in the Pennines between the Snake Pass and Huddersfield. His labours have punctuated the autumn and produced a cheerful account of the two of us at the dining table. We have just committed ourselves to a frame and expect to have it in place by Christmas. We hope it will encourage some of our friends to do likewise. Portrait painters are having a bad time, what with the recession, and ought to be supported.

Last March Renate and EG attended a launch party at Kaiserswerth arranged by the publishers of the memoir of their parents. It was more of a seminar with a series of interesting contributions about the period. The volume itself has been surprisingly well received and the publishers are delighted with the sales, the proceeds of which go to church funds.

The Kaloko Trust is now properly established in its own right and has its London office in Philip's flat. Ronald Prosser, who runs his own printing press in Newport, Gwent, has published a charming account of his visit to Luansobe. If anyone who does not receive a copy with this letter would like one, we are happy to provide this. The continuing drought in Southern Africa affects Zambia as most of the other 'front line' states. The region is now definitely classed as semi, if not wholly, arid. The Kaloko Trust is working hard on ways and means of enabling the inhabitants to live reasonably on what little water there is.

Becca is much happier with the quality of the tuition and supervision at Goldsmith in the second year of her Mus.Bac course. Her interest in composition is getting a chance to develop. Both she and Crispin performed their own compositions at Vernon Thomas' 80th birthday at the Royal Foundation of St. Katherine, in November.

R and EG were able to spend a weekend with Martin in Debrecen during another visit to Hungary in May. As the 'Geneva' of Hungary, the University of Debrecen was founded in the 17th century as the Calvinist theological faculty for the largely reformed region straddling the Hungarian-Romanian frontier. Here is another region where the Church played an important part in bringing about the downfall of Stalinism. It was the reformed Bishop of Timisoara who triggered the liberalisation in Romania in 1989. Martin has been involved in a substantial re-organisation of the university in Drebecen and he flies out to Beijing for Christmas with Janet, they hope to be posted together again when his assignment in Drebecen comes to an end next year.

Crispin's work in the Hallé library continues twice a week. The making up of scores for 106 players in accordance with the relevant conductor's interpretation keeps him pretty busy. At Vigneau earlier in the year Crispin struck up a good relationship with Peter Jarvis, an expatriate clarinettist and composer who now lives near Duras with his wife and children. They and Jeremy Rose, who was staying at Vigneau at the time, put on a very creditable concert for our neighbours and friends.

Rosemarie's work with the University of the Third Age was recognised by her appointment as an honorary life member. She enjoys her teaching there as much as ever. She writes:

On April 13th, Crispin, Thomas and R took the Air-Kenya flight to Lusaka via Nairobi. It is not an airline she would recommend. There were long delays, both in London and Nairobi. However, Philip and Godfridah were at the airport to meet them and they spent a leisurely evening and morning together in a comfortable hotel where Phil and Tom could have a swim in the pool before the started on the 4½ hours drive by landrover to Luansobe. During that time they were told that there would be a wedding reception on April 23rd to celebrate, in a big way, with family and friends Phil and Fridah's wedding. The official ceremony had already taken place a few weeks earlier. This was news indeed, and Chris and R hastened to buy a pair of trousers since C had brought his jeans and shorts only. R's one dress would have to do. Peter and Aggie Moxon, long standing and generous friends, gave the reception at their house and garden. R was glad to meet many more of Phil's friends as well as members of Fridah's RC family. Her sisters and aunts had already arrived the night before and Chris and R had spent the day preparing potato-salad for about 20 people. Aggie had made a fine wedding cake, iced by Peter and we have a photo showing Phil and Fridah standing behind it ready to cut the cake. The friends of Phil R had not met before, were mixed marriage couples where the husbands had come to Zambia in the fifties, either to farm or set up manufacturing plants, and then married Zambian women. She particularly enjoyed meeting Jim Sanderson who told her among other things that Zambia has only two resources: copper and land. The supply of the former is almost exhausted and the land has never been sufficiently developed agriculturally to make Zambia independent of food imports. He was very pessimistic about the future, his own and that of the country. Since then we have met Koni, Sanderson's youngest daughter, who is a student of French and Spanish in our university. Among the guests was Senior Chief Mushili, the patron of Ndola Rural District; and his Councillor. About 6 years ago he gave Phil about 600 acres of land which the latter is gradually turning into an oasis in the middle of the bush.

Every time one visits Luansobe the community has grown. New services and amenities have been added. The new development R and C saw this time is the Health Clinic for Luansobe area with Pat as District Nurse and, Matilda her Assistant, in charge. R attended the Monday Clinic where the young mothers have their infants weighed, vaccinated, injected, eye-drops administered and they themselves are instructed in the methods and importance of birth control. Every day people die of Aids in Zambia.

Crispin was able to carry on teaching the recorder to Joshua and Willard, two young men with whom he began to teach two years ago and who were glad to continue their lessons after work each day, and C enjoyed it also. R and E are now looking forward to having a week with Phil and Fridah at Livingstone, in mid-January in order to have a holiday with them by the Victoria Falls.

R was able to combine the visit to Gorlitz (bordertown on the river

Neisse between Germany and Poland) with a Pilgrim group consisting of British, Dutch and West Germans, with seeing two of her sisters in their homes. Both took part in the visit to Gorlitz from August 5th - 15th. The theme and purpose of the visit was Reconciliation and the chief planners and organisers of the 'Quest' were the East German Pastor Wilfred Baier, a West German Pilgrim and our own leader. We were comfortably housed in the well-appointed Diocesan Centre outside Gorlitz. Friends from East and West Germany and from Poland joined us for part of the time. The latter was the young Pastor Pech and his charming wife from Marpacz. On the days when we stayed in, we had Bible study sessions in the mornings and discussion with various visitors in the afternoon. We also went twice into Gorlitz, a fine medieval city, being busily restored with west German money and expertise. We learned in the discussions with Baier, his wife and other East Germans how difficulty they are finding the fact that West Germany with its material resources and also with great energy and commitment is transforming their society, cities and institutions, but: without much consultations. East Germans know they have not only suffered and endured a great deal but also learned much that is important to them and which they do not want to be forgotten.

The newly elected Protestant bishop of Gorlitz, a West German, spent one afternoon with us. He is well aware of the situation and doing his utmost to encourage dialogue, consultation and joint decisions. We like him very much. The most interesting of our day trips was the one to Karpacz to Pastor Pech's church and parish. The church is an old wooden church from Norway. The youth-group of the parish sang to us in Polish, songs which are well known to, and sung by our own parish youth-groups. We met, over afternoon tea, the young Mayor of Karpacz who shared with us his hopes that his town, in the beautiful foothills of the Riesengebirge, through which one of my sisters had hiked as a young girl, should belong to Poles, Germans and Czechs alike since it is a border region which has changed hands many times during its history. The final witness to our combined desire for reconciliation was the Communion Service in Karpacz Church shared by Pastor Pech and Pastor Gurke, one of our own West German members. For him and two other members of our fellowship the visit to East Germany and Poland had meant a very special personal pilgrimage and quest because they were born there and grew up there.

The project to assess the role of the media in the development of democracy in Africa has occupied EG and his colleagues. He was in Kenya in May and in the Ivory Coast in November. The political evolution of these two countries is surprisingly similar in that both had strong personalities to lead the country to independence. These leaders ran their countries largely as one party states for the first generation or so of independence. On their demise arrangements were made, in line with the Lomé Convention, to democratise the political systems. Multi-party elections were held in the early 1990s and in the Ivory Coast the second democratic general election was held while EG was there. The comparable elections in Kenya are due to be held early in 1997. Both countries now have most of the trappings of democracy, but their politicians are becoming adept at stultifying the democratic arrangements when this suits their political objectives.

Recently Lord George Thomson of Monifieth, who is now chairman of the trustees of Leeds Castle near Maidstone, offered to invite a number of EG's friends and colleagues from the broadcasting organisations and universities to discuss what should go into the book on *The Public Interest in Broadcasting* which he is writing with the help of the Leverhulme Trust. The instability caused by the take-over of many ITV companies by accountants is rubbing off onto the service which these companies provide for their viewers. Nor does it leave the BBC unaffected. Broadcasters compete for a share of the audience. If one channel has more, the others have fewer viewers. The outline of the book is emerging quite well. It remains to fill in the chapters.

In October EG spent a week in Poland to study the media situation there. While he was there he also attended (with his Wyndham Place Trust hat on) part of an evaluation meeting of the Office for Democratic Institutions and Human Rights (LDIHR) of the Organisation for Security and Cooperation in Europe. These are bodies that emerged from the Helsinki accords. EG was much impressed by the way in which government delegations and non-governmental organisations mingled freely at the conference and worked hard to improve the democratic institutions in their respective countries. EG was much heartened by this little publicised but well run international body, headed by Audrey Glover, an ambassador from the FCO. It seems that the development of parliaments, of an independent judiciary and of an accountable executive is proceeding in most Central and East European countries without too many hiccoughs. Altogether a cheering experience.

Back in Manchester the Liberal Democrats are making steady headway on the City Council. They still have about 14 seats to win before they can claim a majority. They hope to achieve this early in the new millennium. With this in view they need to think strategically, as well as to continue the splendid tactical work done by Liberal councillors on the ground. So we have launched the Cobden Club to encourage this. At its first meeting EG was impressed by the quality of the, mainly young, Liberal activists present. It is not easy to make headway against the stalinist tactics of the Labour majority here, who have hardly heard of Tony Blair. So the notion of a Lib-Lab pact has a long way to go here, (as I suspect, in other conurbations). The Wedell contribution to the Liberal Democrat cause is pretty small owing to our other commitments, but we back them as best we can, both here and at Cowley Street.

The 1996 letter

PHILIP'S LETTER TO SHIRLEY LEGGE gives a fuller account of his work in Zambia, which at the time was a country with virtually no cash economy. From 2012 looking back, it is almost incredible that the increase in the price of copper has turned Zambia into a prosperous country. It is also interesting to remember that in 1996 Mozambique joined the Commonwealth, since almost all her neighbours were already members. That showed the resilience of the Commonwealth in the international field at the time. The Chantry Group published *No Discouragement* which proved to be an indicator of much religious thinking that followed in the following years.

18 Cranmer Road
Manchester
M20 0AW

Second Sunday in Advent 1996

As much-put-upon small shareholders of Eurotunnel plc we were not pleased when a load of polystyrene went up in flames inside the tunnel. But we persevere, convinced that our children and grandchildren will be glad of the shares one day. The tunnel is a bit like the whole European enterprise; just as one glimpses a light at the end of the 'tunnel', the next problem looms.

Given the tortuous European issues, it is comforting to turn to basic matters of survival. In that context you may be interested in an extract from a letter Philip wrote to Shirley Legge of the Beatriec Hankey Foundation on 23/10:

> I am back at Kakushi, visiting our settlers here and I am moved to write because I am sure you would be delighted to see the use that they are making of one of the oil presses that the Beatrice Hankey Foundation so generously donated 3 years ago. It is a fine sight; the women, as a group-most of them with ids on their backs - gossiping cheerfully while they take it in turns to operate the

laborious press. Literally oil is what keeps the whole community "liquid" at this time of year; towards the end of the parched dry season, waiting for rains to set in for the main season of cultivation Apart from cooking oil and oil cake for their domestic use and to keep their cattle looking so well, they can barter the surplus for maize which is the staple of barter for everything from soap and salt to clothes and cattle - and hairdos.

Since there is virtually no cash at all in this economy. Kaloko is their main purchasing agent: i.e. we can purchase their surplus of maize and oil cake in return for seed and fertiliser. By this time of year the Kakushi and Luanga streams have stopped flowing, but deep enough pools will remain (until the next rains) to keep the kitchen gardens of cabbages, rape, tomatoes and onions going. Old Mrs Bwalya (the mother of one of our settlers) has swapped 4 chickens for 4 gallons of fertiliser.

We may not be spectacular, but we are establishing secure, self-supporting communities over time. The men are looking very lean, but most of the women and kids look quite buxom. Indeed at the Kwesha site, three of the first group of settlers have built themselves substantial houses; concrete slabs with brick and plaster superstructure, from their own resources.

Here some of the settlers have started their own roof-tile making plant - which in a couple of years will probably become another lucrative unit. I say two years, because it does seem to take that sort of time for these groups to come to terms with managing and maintaining non-traditional activities. The oil press is an example; it has taken them until this season to establish its potential; now they want other ones.

The oxen that we purchased (with the Beatrice Hankey Foundation help) for our village food security programme have been pretty thoroughly trained by now and are posed for work when the rains set in. We will be covering 62 families in 11 villages this year - altogether 580 people. Willard Chitimbo and Freda, my wife, have developed a very thorough schedule of extension visits to ensure that our seed and fertiliser in-puts will fall on well prepared fields.

Martin and Janet continue their long-distance commuting. Janet moved to the University of Hong Kong in September; Martin is hoping to complete this year the structural integration into the University of Debrecen of the teacher training activities for the region. At the same time he is finishing his PhD thesis, which deals with the management aspects of the expansion of higher education. He is spending Christmas in Hong Kong and returns here early in the New Year to see his supervisor before returning to Hungary.

Becca is well into the second half of her Mus. Bas. Course. It is hard work, particularly since she is doing it alongside her teaching and therapeutic activities. But she prefers to be independent and refuses offers of help. Her use of contemporary musical idioms has resulted in some quite complicated compositions, which seem to be well regarded by her peers. She is looking for a larger flat and may pass on 94 Eton Place to Martin, who is looking for a pied-a-terre in central London.

Crispin and we all have lost a good and loyal friend in Jill Rose who died in September. She had celebrated her 70th birthday in the spring and mercifully was ill only a short time. She has left a big gap in the lives of her children, and all of us. The Hallé library where Crispin works, moved to the new Bridgewater Hall in the summer. There the orchestra at long last has a worthy headquarters. The hall is on the banks of the Bridgewater Canal next door to the G-Mex exhibition centre. It is revolutionising concert going in the city. Whether the Mancunians can live up to a much-expanded range of musical offerings remains to be seen.

Among concerts in which Crispin was involved was one at Vigneau for the commune of Lachapelle. John Green, Peter Jarvis and Barbara Seymour contributed. Almost half the adult population of the village turned out, and coped with some quite difficult Poulenc before adjourning for food and drink. The mayor is using the proceeds to encourage village children to stay on at school.

R continues her lecturing for the University of the Third Age. This leads to other lecturing invitations around Manchester and keeps her busy. For both her and EG the year has brought intimations of mortality. R has taken a long time to recover from a fall downstairs at the end of April. She badly bruised her right upper arm and shoulder and it has taken until now to regain most of the use of the arm. Being right-handed she tends to use the arm more energetically than she should. But the year has also brought rewarding and happy times. In May she and Martin met in Passau, an old city in Bavaria at the confluence of the Danube, Inn and Itzel rivers. They spent an enjoyable and interesting weekend together. En route R had two nights with her sister and brother-in-law in Heidelberg, another beautiful town, and stopped for lunch with Georg and Leda Luyken in Munich. She much enjoyed the train journey through that southern region of Germany. We also had our summer break at Calpe as usual, though R was reduced to paddling rather than swimming, and with EG not really well enough to make the best of it.

Ten happy and carefree days in Ottawa in August with two of her fellow students with whom she had shared a dormitory from 1943-46 at the Wistow Training College, was a real treat. Olga and Leonore had emigrated to Canada after the war. Between them the three released an amazing stream of memories. Ottawa is a most attractive capital city, surrounded by water and forests. The government buildings on parliament Hill with their Gothic towers and turrets create, from the distance, a fairy-tale effect. The city has a marvellous modern Art Gallery and the Canadian Museum of Civilisation with an interesting section on native Canadian art.

R had the feeling that Canada is growing towards the discovery of her own identity and trying to reconcile the culture and life of her indigenous peoples with 'new comers' and their history and scale of values. Canada strikes her as more humane than the USA. Even modern Ottawa at the bottom of Parliament Hill, built of glass, steel and concrete, has a human dimension to it. The wide and straight avenues, with shops on either side, have a broad section right through the middle with trees, seats and tables and small tea/coffee stalls: all very agreeable. With Olga, Leonore and her husband, R was taken out into the attractive countryside. She will have to go again to see more of that huge country. Her first visit to Canada has left her with a sense of real enjoyment and appreciation.

Having done the case studies of the Ivory Coast and Kenya in 1995 EG spent time in Mozambique in the spring. After 17 years of civil war since independence the country is just beginning to get back on its feet. Surrounded as it is by Commonwealth countries, it decided to join the club in January, at the same time as the Cameroons in West Africa. Let no one say the Commonwealth is dead! The final report on the media and democracy in Africa has now gone to the European Commission. It will be published by John Libbey in the New Year. So EG has turned back to the Leverhulme-Trust supported book on *The Public Interest in Broadcasting* on which he started two years ago. Macmillans will publish this together with the St Martin's Press in the US. So now all the remains to be done is to write the book.

Following the completion of James Mark's substantial essay on the nature of faith, about a dozen of the members of the Chantry Group have now produced companion pieces. Together they make an interesting collection of pieces on the evolution of theological thinking and attitudes to organised religion over the last 40 years or so. It is, as far as we know, the only attempt to do this by a group of people with no professional or ecclesiastical axe to grind. So we think it might, warts and all, be useful to some of our contemporaries who have lived through the same time-span. At present we are waiting to hear whether any publisher is interested.

The 1997 letter

THE SHIFT IN GOVERNMENT from the Tories to the Labour Party clearly pleases us. The "hard-faced egotism of the Thatcher years" was at long last over. Its long term effects remain to this day. The production of a new coat of arms to consolidate the two earlier ones in Rosemarie's and my families was significant. The Wedell motto *beneficium sit* proved to be useful (Genesis 12.2).

18 Cranmer Road
Manchester
M20 0AW

Second Sunday in Advent 1997

The massive political *boulversement* on May Day this year continues to reverberate around our lives. It is not so much that the Labour Party won, but that at long last the hard-faced egotism of the Thatcher years seems to be yielding to a more humane and sharing approach to the organisation of our common life. How much of the extraordinary recovery of civilised common sense manifested in the early indications of the new government policies will survive the harsh realities remains to be seen. But we are grateful that once again sensible options are available in many areas of public life.

We are now, of course, relatively passive onlookers of these changes. We are glad that the Liberal Democrats are adopting a stance of a critical friend of the new administration Their relatively cosy relationship to the Labour leadership in London is not reflected in many of the northern conurbations, where the Liberal Democrats are the only opposition to well entrenched and complacent Labour majorities in the town halls. So we do our best to support the efforts towards sensible electoral reform which seems to us to be the precondition of a more adult political environment in future.

Martin and Philip are, by virtue of their jobs, more involved in public affairs in their respective spheres. Martin is in his fourth year at Debrecen, seeing through the substantial reorganisation of the higher education system in Hungary. The re-establishment of democracy of some sort in Hungary has brought with it the will to modernise the country's institutions, as in most other central European countries. The British Council seems to be playing an important part in this modernisation, and its (relatively) young "experts" from this country are making a solid contribution to this process. Janet is similarly engaged in the modernisation process in Hong King. Martin went out for the handover of the colony to China; they are both reasonably confident that open systems will survive in spite of the bluster preceding the handover.

It was good to have Philip and Freda for two and half months in the summer. We had the best part of a fortnight together in Calpe in July, and a family weekend altogether around Crispin's birthday at the beginning of August. That was a rare treat. Philip's Kaloko Trust has been taking on a wider developmental role in the Ndola Rural District in Zambia. It is evident that the extension of the various Luansobe projects into the neighbouring villages is now gaining in significance. We enclose a copy of the 1996 report of the Trust rather than taking up too much space in this letter. What is evident is the excellent start made by the UK Trust for Kaloko in backing this imaginative enterprise.

Rebecca gave up 94 Eton Place to Martin in the course of the summer and moved in with Shulamit for the last year of her Mus. Bac course at Goldsmith's College. The flat is much nearer New Cross and saves her a lot of travelling time. The composition part of the course is what really engages her. We hope that she does well enough to be able, one way or another, to develop her work in the academic field.

Crispin is trying to be more outgoing than before since Jill Rose died last year. Alas, he lost, as we all did, another good friend of many years' standing in Margaret Thomas who died in October. Barry Hodson, his clarinet tutor, retired and moved to Anglesey in the summer. He has been replaced by Jennifer Brown, a lively final year student at the RNCM. David Morgan, Crispin's pianist friend, came down to Vigneau in September in order to help with the village concert, which once again attracted a substantial audience. We are well impressed with our new young mayor, who has introduced some street lighting (four street lamps to be precise) as well as creating a library for the village children with the proceeds of our concerts.

The book by members of the Chantry Group is now out and we enclose a flier for *No Discouragement*. The Group has been quite a significant element in our lives since we set up house in London in 1950. At that time we began to give coffee parties to talk about God and the world. The first chapter of the book recounts how these meetings have developed over the last forty-five years or so. Over this time our theological views have been modified, in some cases quite sharply. But we have managed to remain friends. James Mark's paper on the nature of faith was read to us in several versions over the years. So it came to be the centre piece of the book, together with contributions from the rest of us. The most difficult chapter was the last, where it would have been agreeable to set down firm conclusions. But life is not like that. We have however been able to indicate certain stances we have in common and which, we hope, can take us into the future. If you would like a copy please let us know.

EG is still struggling with the book on *The Public Interest in Broadcasting*. Macmillans have kindly extended the deadline, so he hopes to finish it in the early part of next year. One of the problems is the volatility of the media industry. It is difficult to know from one month to the next what structural and economic changes are likely to take place. So EG is inclined to concentrate on the ontological issues which need to determine the future of the media.

The College of Arms in Queen Victoria Street has been helping us to consolidate two coats of arms which have been used in or families since the late 15th century and to bring them up to date. Clarenceux King of Arms has now produced the armorial ensigns at the head of this letter and they have been agreed by the Earl Marshal. They contain the Wedell motto: *beneficium sit*, or *be a blessing*, taken from Genesis 12, verse 2; the beanstalk of the Bonhoeffer arms which appears first on the seal with which Claes van den Boenhoff in 1479 sealed documents now in the archives of the city of Nymegen in the Netherland; the dove from the Sack family arms of R's mother, first documented in Nordhausen in Germany about 1480, the white horse of Hanover illustrating the Anglo-Hanoverian connection of the Meyer family which began during the condominium from 1714-1837 and has continued to the present day; the rising sun of knowledge from the arms of Victoria University of Manchester; the symbolic bridge illustrating the bridge-building propensities of members of the family across various divides. The arms are, of course, of no immediate practical use. But we think they give an historical dimension to the doings of these families over the last half-millennium and, brought up to date, may be of encouragement to our successors.

Rosemarie spent three weeks in Zambia with Thomas at Easter. This was her third visit, going over at two year intervals. Every time there are new developments to admire. This time new classrooms were going to take in the senior pupils from the junior section i.e. secondary classroom provision.

The school has a new headmaster whose wife is also a teacher of Domestic Science. They, with 'our own' Odness, wife of Philip's senior assistant, should form a good nucleus for the other Government teachers to work with. The school is mainly supported by the International Children's Trust with whom Philip worked also in India. They have created a Sponsorship Scheme whereby a sponsor in this country pays for a child's school education and weekly boarding. R has sponsored a pupil there and enjoys seeing her on her visits. The Kaloko agricultural team has extended its work into the surrounding region trying to educate the hunter-gatherer mentality for real agricultural and ecological awareness and skills. In this way they are aiming to help Zambians to move to a new stage of development. That is hard and slow work.

Overall, the Kaloko community is committed to its 'village', another new phenomenon because rural Africans live in small clumps of 3-4 huts spread out over an area which does not encourage community development. So Tim Godfrey, who joined Kaloko last September, sees his work in terms of helping the Kaloko villagers to learn to see themselves as neighbours and partners, and to establish a community spirit and encourage their own identity. Almost three years ago the Ventham family: Tom, Julia and Barney joined the Kaloko team. Tom has taken over the management of the building projects and Julia has helped to develop the crèche. She also helps with teaching in the school. Tim has found them to be good friends.

The U3A group in Stockport has started for another autumn and spring term, which keeps R on her toes. She spent a long weekend with Becca in the guest house of the Abbey of the Burnham Sisters in early November. This gave them time to talk and walk, and for Becca to finish a composition. They also re-established their contact with their special Sisters.

36. Eberhard and Renate at Meilhan on the Canal Laterale.

37. Hannah and her children come to lunch.

38. The Winckler sisters at Gudrun's house.

39. Supper at Vigneau, Summer 2010 with Rosemarie, EGW, Crispin, Shulamit, Lina, Chanya, Kathy Wedell, Stuart White and Isaac.

40. Crispin between Simon and Jane.

41. Cousins at the Christmas Theatre Party at the Royal Exchange, 1994.

42. Cousins at the Christmas Theatre Party at the Royal Exchange, 1996.

43. Family Brunch with Klaus and Nina.

44. Family Brunch: Nina and Martin and Philip.

45. Nephews and Nieces at our Diamond Wedding Celebration 31 May 2008: (L to R):
Crispin Wedell, Kathy Wedell, Andrew Lockley, Philip Wedell, Simon Lockley, Hannah Rocholl,
Stephen Wedell, and Maria Rocholl.

The 1998 letter

T HE GIBBON QUOTATION from *The Decline and Fall of the Roman Empire* seemed apt at the time. In the event we were not on the verge of the emergence of Europe "as one Republic". In 2012 we seem to be further from that in the UK than ever. The need to reprint *No Discouragement* suggests that our ideas were of interest.

> 18 Cranmer Road
> Manchester
> M20 0AW

Second Sunday in Advent 1998

It is the duty of the patriot to prefer and promote the exclusive and glory of his native country: but a philosopher may be permitted to enlarge his views and to consider Europe as one great republic, whose various inhabitants have attained almost the same level of politeness and cultivation. The balance of power will continue to fluctuate, and the prosperity of our own, or the neighbouring kingdoms, may be alternatively exalted or depressed: but these partial events cannot essentially injure our general state of happiness, the system of arts, and laws, and manners, which so advantageously distinguish, above the rest of mankind, the Europeans.

> Edward Gibbon, *The Decline and Fall of the Roman Empire*
> Vol. VI, chapter XXXVIII, p, 402 (1818 edition)

We thought the quotation from Edward Gibbon would make a good opening to this year's Christmas letter, because we do seem to be on the verge of the emergence of Europe "as one republic". That being so, it would be a comfort to know that its inhabitants "have attained almost the same level of politeness and cultivation". But then (EG in particular) could not help recalling that exactly sixty years ago he witnessed unimaginable acts of savagery as Jews in Germany were hounded out of house and home. Since then comparable acts of savagery have occurred in Northern Ireland, in Bosnia & Kosovo, not to speak of the Holocaust and the atrocities of wartime.

So what price politeness and cultivation now? We have, we think, to hold on to the fact that in all these situations there are just and courageous men and women who stand out against cruelty and injustice; who are willing at the cost of their own lives to stand up for those under attack. Bernefield the greengrocer, Korle the driver, Homan the pastor, Salzmann the dentist: they were the heroes of the *Kristallnacht* of 1938[3] who justify our claim to politeness and cultivation. They distinguish, above the rest of mankind, the Europeans.

Our lives in middle England have fortunately been relatively godly and quiet. For that we are immensely grateful. Such gratitude is particularly appropriate after fifty years of married life which we completed earlier in the year. In July many of you were able to join us for a celebration at Chancellor's House, the University splendid new residential centre in Fallowfield. About 120 people from many parts of the country and of Europe joined in the celebrations. They represented most phases of our life together. Only the University's limits on accommodation prevented us from inviting all those we would have liked to be there. On the Sunday morning we held a colloquium on the next fifty years. This produced a lot of interesting contributions, some more serious than others.

Over Easter Martin and Philip invited us to do a tour of the Antipodes. Here we enjoyed seeing several old friends who are too far away for normal contact. Inge Ghosh came fro Ottawa to take care of Crispin and the household. In Australia Barbara Williams came down to Sydney from Brisbane to help us to find our way. It was a great joy to see her again after many years. John Wren-Lewis welcomed us to the University of Sydney. Some of you will remember him as a lively lay theologian in London in the 1950s. In New Zealand Peter and Gaby Dane welcomed us to their splendid house overlooking the Bay of Islands. Werner Pelz came over from Melbourne to join the party. He has now retired from the University there and his second wife Mary is, alas, no longer. Peter Dane has also retired from the English Department of the University of Auckland. He and Gaby are surrounded by their sizeable family, as well as growing lots of exotic fruit on their estate. We regarded the whole trip as a holiday, and did not attempt to do any research. So that was a splendid golden wedding present.

After the party at Chancellor's House we had some weeks at Vigneau

---

[3] See Wedell, *A Memoir of Troubled Times* p 54-58

when members of the family came and went so that we could see something of each other at greater leisure. Martin and Janet were both home.

Martin concluded his work in Debrecen. In September he was appointed to a senior lectureship in Applied Linguistics in the University of Leeds, the first time he had applied for a university post at home. He is also responsible for developing a dependence of the University at Leeds intended to turn the teaching force in Hong Kong into a graduate profession. This gives him responsibilities in Hong Kong which are particularly convenient since Janet is still there for another two years. They have now bought a flat in Leeds within five minutes of the University and it looks as though he will be pretty stretched and happy there.

Crispin's life continues with more responsibility which he seems to enjoy. He, Rebecca, Rachel Barlow and their friends David Morgan and Jeremy Rose took responsibility for the musical side of the gold wedding party. This was full of interesting items and ended with general dancing to a band assembled by Jeremy. Becca's singing of the WH Auden song *Tell me the truth about love* set to music by Benjamin Britten brought the house down.

Becca completed her Mus.Bac. at Goldsmith's college this summer with a good degree. As a result of this she has been awarded a scholarship giving her access to one of the composers of the Contemporary Music Network. So her composing career is gaining substance. She and Shulamit are happy in their flat at Camberwell Green. We see quite a lot of them since one or the other tends to be here often. Shulamit has some responsibility for the training of speech therapists, which appears to be concentrated in the University here.

We were much delighted to have Philip and Frieda here again for two and half months or so in the summer. They brought Thomas down to Vigneau at the same time as the Simon Lockleys from Yorkshire were there with their three children. So we had a lively party cycling along the Canal du Midi and canoeing down the Dropt near Alemans. Philip is thinking of taking a sabbatical next year in order to do some advanced work at the School of Oriental and African Studies, his alma mater. At a time when the work of Kaloko is expanding fast it is not easy to get away. We are sure, though, that after ten years in Zambia, he does need to allow time to think and to replenish his intellectual and emotional resources.

An attack of flu laid us all low at the beginning of December. Crispin led the way with a high temperature and bronchial cough, followed immediately by EG and then R. A week or so later we are all up again but still weak, and are looking forward to recovering fully over Christmas near the Klaus' in Herefordshire. R thinks that age and diminishing energy may be pointing towards retirement from her University of the Third Age teaching commitment. She wants to have time to work on various diaries of her overseas journeys and some of her early writings. So she intends to say goodbye to the splendid group of U3A friends. After Christmas she will begin to prepare for her next visit to Zambia at Easter. She will take Tom along to spend his holidays with Philip.

The collection of essays called *No Discouragement*, a flyer about which we enclosed last year quite soon exhausted the first printing. A second printing with minor corrections has now come out. Alas, James Mark who had the most substantial piece in it has this year become very frail and now lives near his daughter in Saffron Waldon. Dorothy Emmet is well established at the Hope Residential Home in Cambridge. Her sight is her main problem. After the sad death of Phyllis Bliss, Rupert has now moved to live near his daughter in Somerset. So the Chantry Group is feeling its age. So far it still contains about twenty of us. We have just looked into the Christian Socialist credentials of the present government at our winter meeting at the Royal Foundation of St Katherine in Stepney.

At Vigneau, Armand and Marie-Rose Poletto retired during the year. They have been succeeded by Richard and Liz Gower, who live just the other side of Seyches. They have been in the area for eight or nine years and make a business of looking after the houses of people like us. We much look forward to their ministrations. The house now has a large hot water supply, as well as a much quieter and more efficient central heating, a boon for those who stay there as well as for ourselves. We hope the palm trees by the pool will survive the present cold spell.

The 1999 letter

ROSEMARIE CAME UNDER the influence of Don Cupitt at this time and moved towards his interpretation of the nature of religious experience. EG managed to deliver the manuscript of *Television at the Crossroads* to McMillan's. The Wyndham Place Trust merged with the Charlemagne Institute and Sir Michael Franklin joined EG as Joint Chairman.

18 Cranmer Road
Manchester
M20 0AW

Advent 1999

The other day a letter arrived from a young Rumanian veterinary surgeon whom we helped in a small way to emigrate to Canada two years ago. He is now a long distance truck driver and writes (sic) "I'm driving a machine - capitalist society have no tender fillings, and I don't have a social life. I always ask myself if it was worth it to leave my country and to have this kind of life… and I can say it worth it. I build my future now, and in two years I'll be a Canadian citizen with a passport to the freedom world". This is a useful reminder for us of the vast number of people around the world who this Christmas are struggling to make a better life for themselves in the open society we have created.

We are having an early family Christmas next weekend because Martin and Philip will be leaving the country. Martin is joining Janet in Hong Kong for Christmas and to see in the new millennium. Then he goes onto Oman to advise the government there how to turn its teachers into a graduate profession, before returning for the new term in Leeds. His PhD thesis is almost completed.

Crispin recently performed with Jeremy Rose at the Wilmslow Guild, where Roger, his harmony tutor runs a choir in which he enjoys singing. In my day the University used to give the Guild a lot of help-in-kind by way of lecturing and tutorial staff. It has now given that up and only helps with courses for qualifications. Adult education has, as a consequence, ceased to be available to rich and poor alike - more's the pity.

Philip on his sabbatical is much immersed in the Development Economics MA at the School of Oriental & African Studies. He is curious to discover how twenty years of practice in South India and Zambia compare with the theory they teach at SOAS. He is also spending the Christmas vacation looking after things in Zambia, and will then bring Freda back here for a while.

Becca has also begun a Master's degree course in Composition at the Guildhall School of Music in London. She has also been "apprenticed" to an established composer under an Arts Council Scheme. That has been a good experience of practical musical creation. She and Shulamit still have the flat in Camberwell Green, which suits them well.

Rosemarie is editing her travel diaries in India, China and Zambia, as well as the journeys she and EG have done together over the years. These accounts have the immediacy of unclouded by vision, and will no doubt delight both old and young when they see the light of day. After that some early diaries produced in the 1930's will be tackled. Meanwhile her quest for "The meaning of it all" in the evolving human history, continues to be stimulated by Don Cuppitt's latest writings: a trilogy of which two slim volumes are out: *The new Religion of life in everyday speech* and *The Meaning of it all in everyday speech*. They are exhilarating and, to her mind, a break with the metaphysics of supernatural religion. They penetrate instead the human everyday world and its natural surroundings with a new understanding of treasures hidden in the 'ordinariness' of our earthly life. There are, of course, other writers and thinkers engaged in similar tasks here and among our fellow-Europeans. John Bowden of the SCM Press keeps remarkably up-to-date with what is going on in Holland and Germany, and with the attempts being made there to describe what a "religionless Christianity" is all about. He translates their books from German and Dutch.

EG has promised Macmillan's to deliver at long last the manuscript of *Television at the Crossroads*. Bryan Luckham has come to his aid as a co-author, and they have now finished ten of the eleven chapters. EG intends to lighten the somewhat heavy text with some witty cartoons by Miloslav Bartak, the brilliant Czech artist.

The Wyndham Place Trust celebrated its fortieth birthday in the autumn, not long after the last of its founders, Trevor Huddleston, died. George Macleod, Alan Booth, Monica Wingate and Douglas Sanders were the other founders, who foresaw the need for an ethical foreign policy long before the present government did; and recognised that the faith communities must promote and monitor it. The intervening decades have proved the wisdom of our founders. Earlier in the year the Charlemagne Institute, founded more recently by some of our ex-Brussels colleagues with a more specifically European orientation, proposed that we should merge. That was done at the end of October, and we go forward together as the Wyndham Place Charlemagne Trust. Sir Michael Franklin and EG carry on as joint chairman for the time being.

Crispin and Rosemarie have, as usual, their annual season tickets for the Hallé concert season at the new Bridgewater Hall and for the Manchester Chamber concert series at the Royal Northern College of Music. In this way they keep in touch with the world of music and its great performers.

The 2000 letter

THE CONTINUING INTEREST in *No Discouragement* was welcome, particularly the understanding that our book had been written not by clergymen but by lay people. As George Pattison wrote:

> One might however ... suggest that the collective authority of the Chantry Group - yes, "authority" - comes precisely from the willingness of people who have borne the burden of trying to live out Christianity in the midst of contemporary public life to testify ... to its continuing importance, indeed centrality in their lives.

For Crispin, 2000 marked the move to Clozapine, which was remarkably effective.

18 Cranmer Road
Manchester
M20 0AW

Advent 2000

In the Spring we had some useful comment on *No Discouragement: Exploring Faith* in the Chantry Group. George Pattison, the Dean of King' College, Cambridge, in Modern Believing, volume 41, No. 1, wrote:

> The latest trends in theological fashion promise a return to robust assertiveness, albeit one mediated by the encounter with post modernity: From the standpoint of 'radical orthodoxy', this and the other essays in this collection would probably appear to be no more than typical examples of liberal whingeing. One might, however, take the opposite view and suggest that the collective authority of the Chantry Group - yes, 'authority' - comes precisely from the willingness of people who have borne the burden of trying to live out Christianity in the midst of contemporary public life to testify both to the rough - or loose-edgedness of their resulting 'theology', but also to its continuing importance and, indeed,

centrality in their lives. Thinking about a collection such as this, then, might suggest - it does to me - that 'authority' in theology today cannot be a matter of buying into a certain intellectual programme, but of working out, in fear and trembling (and occasional joy) the words that work, that do not entrap us in double-think but seem to enable us to help one another that one step further along our difficult and unmapped road. What such 'authority' underwrites may seem to be a little more than scraps, fragments, and hints; but if these turn out to be enough to sustain a life, what more should we want?".

Charles Handy of the London Business School had earlier "found this collection of credos stimulating, irritating, over my head and comforting in turn. If this group of wise and successful individuals can disagree about the nature of faith, but still feel it important to say what they believe, then I am both encouraged and licensed to do likewise. The essays here are an imperative to contemplation about the meaning of our humanity."

As members of the Group we were interested by the response which seemed to understand what we have been about all these years. The Group started in our flat in Lower Belgrave Street in 1952 and has held together with comings and goings, for the last fifty years.

The rest of the family has looked benevolently on our eccentricities, as they have pursued their respective vocations. Becca completed the masters course in Composition at the Guidhall School in the summer, and only just missed a first. She has been appointed composer-in-residence at the University of Coleraine in Northern Ireland in the spring. We shall be interested to hear what music emerges from this assignment.

Philip is in the second year of his half-time sabbatical at the School of Oriental and African Studies. The development theory they teach there differs markedly from the reality on the ground in Zambia. Philip is willing to see to what extent these conflicting concepts can be harmonised. He has been commuting to Zambia and Freda has spent a large portion of this time with him in London. She now faces a gynaecological operation. Phil sees a lot of Tom and they enjoy their weekends together.

Crispin has, on the whole benefited from the shift from Fluphenazine to Clozapine, which was begun earlier in the year. The problem has been the shortage of consultants in the NHS to monitor the new medication. Since March Crispin has had four consecutive specialists, each one only a locum. We hope that the fifth will be permanent. However, already the January consultation has been postponed.

On the musical front Crispin has benefited from Joanne Patton, his clarinet tutor, who is a gifted player with the Hallé, as well as an excellent teacher. He has also joined Roger Wilks' choir and very much enjoys it. R and he have season tickets for the Hallé and the RNCM chamber concerts.

Martin completed his PhD thesis with flying colours in the summer. At present he is much taken up with the academic demands of the University. He also advises the Oman government on the methods of turning its teachers into a graduate profession For Christmas he and Janet will be together in Hong Kong.

R has been able to get her many travel diaries sorted, typed and partly edited. However, since last March she has been preoccupied with the restlessness and fidgeting which Crispin's new drug Clozapine has produced. Clozapine has also brought positive results for which we are, of course, thankful. Nevertheless, the strain has been considerable. R's arthritis has reduced her mobility and she can move only slowly at present.

Having Martin and Philip at home is a great joy and we appreciate their weekend visits. Rebecca has just now succeeded Philip for a long weekend in Manchester and Martin comes over the for odd Saturday or Sunday brunch.

We are profoundly thankful that the terrible flood ordeals experienced in other parts of the country have not affected us in any serious manner. Our house and garden are standing up well to the excessive rainfalls of this autumn and winter.

EG's book on *Television at the Crossroads* is at long last in the press. Brian Luckham has joined EG as co-author. Macmillans expect to publish next summer. They and St Martin's Press in the USA have now combined into a global imprint called **Palgrave**. The sorting out of the new editorial arrangements has delayed things, but may turn out to be worthwhile in view of the world-wide coverage which it will bring. We are cheering up the text with Miroslov Bartack's splendid cartoons which enliven the head of each chapter (see below). The government White Paper on Communications Policy is just out. We think the Secretary of State inclines to our view, but cannot resist the pressure of the commercial interests. So our conclusion will remain on record, that there is hope for television only if the workers in the industry establish their own version of the Hippocratic Oath.

The 2001 letter

TELEVISION AT THE CROSSROADS was published and did quite well. My notion of an "Hippocratic oath" for broadcasters did not catch on, alas.

18 Cranmer Road
Manchester
M20 0AW

Advent 2001

We were in France in September at the time of the World Trade Centre bombings. So the impact on us was moderated by the requirements of the Vendange, one of the more permanent and timeless events of the year in the Lot et Garonne. The fact that some people were prepared to commit suicide at such a time was registered as an inconsiderate attempt to divert attention from these important events. At the persistence of the dislocation and the consequent preoccupation with attempts to "get even" with world terrorism have been difficult to evade in the press and on television. That, together with an unpleasant disagreement about the use of the Beatrice Hankey Foundation surpluses has rather spoilt what was to have been our first autumn without substantial writing commitments.

On the health front Rosemarie has had considerable trouble with arthritic hips and knees. She writes:

> However, I derive much joy from looking out of my study window at the trees, shrubs and still-flowering roses, at the changing and often grey sky, and at the variety of birds from large wood pigeons to magpies, from thrush and blackbirds to tiny swift tits and robins, occasionally scattered by greedy, restless squirrels.
> I cannot but marvel at nature's manifold expressions of living beings of which I and all my fellow human beings are the culminations: 'the highest form of consciousness in the universe' according to Buddha. Above all I am conscious

of the teaching and example of Jesus in his closeness to nature, so wonderfully expressed by him in his parables from nature.

It now seems best to replace at least one hip joint after Christmas. We both look forward to a significant amelioration of the condition from that. Our surgeon at the Alexandra Hospital and the anaesthetist take these operations in their stride. So we are well placed for a good job. We hope that by Easter R will be a new woman.

Crispin continues to thrive on Clozapine which is progressively enabling him to take control of his lifestyle. That is just a well because the NHS shortage of psychiatrists continues, as last year, to inhibit his treatment. We can only hope for better continuity of the medical staff next year. In the meantime Cris has decided to take Spanish more seriously - The Spanish Government has bucked the trend by increasing its cultural expenditure. Unlike the French Cultural Delegation and the Goethe Institute, which have all but closed, we now have a flourishing Instituto Cervantes, and Cris is benefiting from that.

In the Spring Becca made the most of her time as composer-in-residence in the University of Coleraine. But the tenure was too short to do much work of substance. So her visit to N. Ireland did not do much more than give her a taste of life in the province. At present she is in Jerusalem and benefiting from work with the composers at the Conservatoire and absorbing the many-facetted cultural life which persists not withstanding the political tensions. We hope she will come back with a better understanding of the things which do not make for peace there.

Martin is in and out, driving over from the University of Leeds where he is now Director of the International Programme of the School of Education. That involves demanding work in China, helping the province of Canton to do the impossible, that is to have all primary schools teaching English by 2003. Since this involves passing through Hong Kong at fairly regular intervals, he and Janet have no problems over keeping in close touch. Martin's other chore, turning the teaching force of Oman into a graduate profession, is well on the way.

Philip finished his part-time M.Sc (Econ) at the School of Oriental and African Studies in September. He has now been appointed Chief Executive of the International Childrens' Trust as well as of the Kaloko Trust. This makes sense because they have the same origins and Philip will be based in England. But the job requires Philip to do a lot more travel, to Mexico and Madras as well as Zambia. He hopes in the New year to combine the offices of the two trusts and possibly to move to share a flat or a house with Crispin in Manchester. In Zambia he is dividing the estate he was left by

Major Moxon, which helps women who are running their own enterprises to create production units. Thomas is in his last year at St Andrews and will go to Eastbourne College in September 2002. He tends to spend his half-terms here, flying up and down via Gatwick and Ringway.

Television at the Crossroads was published in June and seems to be doing quite well. The economics of publishing are curious: hardback editions are priced expensively. A paperback edition may follow if the demand justifies it. That is a decision we await in the next month or so. The notion in the book of an 'Hippocratic oath' has not caught on up to now. The problem is that the creative people are more than ever dependant on the patronage of the BBC and the independent production companies. They for their part, are not anxious to let producers off the leash. At least the idea of the personal responsibility of the creative people has now been floated, and can be picked up when the time is ripe. I feel I have now completed the work I began in 1960.

The 2002 letter

ROSEMARIE WROTE THAT she had outgrown religion and reached human adulthood. She wrote, "I have the greatest respect and thankfulness for the Buddha, for Jesus, Mahatma Ghandi and the great religious geniuses throughout human history." Coming from her, this caused a fair amount of fluttering in the dovecotes of her friends.

EG's attempts to give some help to the organisation supporting asylum seekers was limited by his health. A series of mini strokes laid him low for some time.

18 Cranmer Road
Manchester
M20 0AW

Advent 2002

This year has been difficult for Rosemarie since the break of her right wrist just before last Christmas delayed the hip joint replacement until Ester. In the end that went well and she is now without pain on her left side. The right knee and hip are wating to be done as soon as an extraordinary mishap has healed. She broke the left wrist also five weeks ago. Fortunately Nick Kenny our surgeon is competent and trained in the latest techniques. So we hope that she will be much restored by the summer. She writes:

> I am really handicapped at the moment and it is a struggle to keep going. The Social Services provide regular help with dressing/undressing and having a shower from Monday to Friday. So life goes on with the preparation of the Advent and Christmas season.
> I am profoundly thankful that most of the family now live near enough to visit and join us for a meal and to stay the night. In this way we remain in close touch. This Advent Sunday we were all together, apart from Becca who is still in Jerusalem, her friend Shulamit was also here for three nights having duties

with the local Jewish Reformed Synagogue. Martin came over for the day from Leeds, and Freda and Phil joined us in the afternoon. At the end of this week they leave for Zambia, so I must get some presents and cards ready for Frieda to take.

In my own faith journey I have reached the point where I have outgrown religion and reached human adulthood. I have the greatest respect and thankfulness for Buddha, for Jesus, Mahatma Gandhi and the great religious geniuses throughout human history. I continue to take great pleasure and comfort from mother nature i.e. the garden, the trees, birds and squirrels, daily affirming my oneness with them.

Our preoccupation with medical matters have prevented much concern with the larger canvas of life around us. The Commonwealth Games were here in July and August, and seem to have gone well. The bill will no doubt come when our local rates are fixed for next year. Tom and his cousins from York and Sheffield came for the opening ceremony, and we also, with the Lukyens, watched the finals of the high jump of the swimming competition. The city was tidied up for the occasion: quite a feat, given the backlog of neglected neighbourhoods.

We were at Vigneau in March and September which are months when the weather is much ahead of Manchester so we enjoyed having our godson Ruprecht Poensgen and his wife and children with us, as well as John and Nora Elliot on their annual visit. The Milligans and other three-tier families also used the house, which was, as a consequence, choc-a-block during the school holidays.

EG has felt for some time that we should do something to help the asylum seekers to adapt to this country. This evidently is, going to be an ongoing need now that travel has become a relatively low-cost commodity, and television allows people to see how the other half lives. People on less-favoured part of the world see the relatively affluent lifestyles in other parts of the world, and do not understand why they should not have a share in them. This is part of the globalisation process, and Asylum seekers are a subset of this global increase in mobility. Although those who are in danger of violence or of danger to life and limb should have priority over economic migrants who move in order to improve their circumstances, the distinction ceases to be significant when the conditions of life in the country of origin expose their citizens to suffering and hardship. So we need to learn to live with migrants, recognising that today's refuges are likely to be tomorrows' citizens and contributors to our national product.

Crispin, in addition to his other 'good works' has started to help Oxfam to run their Didsbury shop. Martin is now in charge of the international work of the Faculty of Education in Leeds, which coincides with the sudden increase of Chinese students at UK universities. How Chinese parents are able to afford costs of up to £50,000 for a first degree is a mystery still to be revealed. Janet continues her work in Hong Kong and they commute between the two cities. Philip and Freda have bought a new house in Northenden, across the Mersey from Didsbury and intend to spend two thirds of their time in Zambia but keep a firm base here at home. Becca and Shulamit survived an academic year in Jerusalem. Becca developed her composing work at the Jerusalem Conservatoire with the aid of a distinguished ex-Russian professor.

In October the children clubbed together to give EG a 75th birthday lunch at Chancellor's house. All the younger generation came, as well as some of the older relations and family friends. Both R and EG were much touched by this manifestation of family togetherness. As somebody said, we did not know there were so many Wedells and Lockleys around.

The 2003 letter

THE Lib Dems were doing well. Audrey Jones became the first Lib Dem Lord Mayor of Manchester, and the Party appeared to be on the way to majority on the City Council. Martin retired from the British Council and was appointed as Head of the International Division of the Education Faculty of the University of Leeds. That brought him pleasantly near to us. EG took the lead in consolidating the Samuel Meyer of Hanover connection. Samuel and Lena had fifteen children, of whom thirteen survived to adulthood. In spite of the Nazi's efforts to extinguish them there are now about five hundred around the world.

18 Cranmer Road
Manchester
M20 0AW

Advent 2003

It seems that our virtually two years of hospitalization are over for the time being. Rosemarie's right hip replacement is as well bedded down as the left so that she is almost back to normal. She now uses a stick only part of the time, and has begun to drive the car again. So we look with some confidence to the years ahead.

This is just as well since the socio-political outlook is very mixed. The government went into Iraq as the junior partner of an Anglo-American attempt to oust the Saddam regime there. The final outcome is by no means evident as we write. The Conservative party are by no criterion an effective opposition. The Lib Dems have been doing well. They now need more experience to turn them into an effective replacement of the Tories on the opposition front bench. At the local level the party is reaping the benefit of some experience. Manchester has in Audrey Jones the first Lib Dem Lord Mayor for decades. And we hope for consolidation of the party's position as it learns to operate as the official opposition on the City Council. A suggestion in *The Independent* that Kenneth Clark should take the pro-European Tories en block into a coalition with the Lib Dems is unlikely to be pursued unless the new Tory leader turns out to be less even-handed than he promised. And it looks as though the voters are not keen to be hurried either over the Euro or over the draft constitution.

Rosemarie has been thinking more about her confident assertion in last Christmas letter that she had 'outgrown religion and reached human adulthood'. Some of her friends have queried that phrase, but she is inclined to stand by it because she is very aware of her own development in these latter years. Her several visits to, and travelling in, India and China have contributed to it.

"We grow through various stages towards human adulthood and one of them is religion. With its definitive claims about the being and person of God, the divine dimension within which all human, animal and vegetable life exists, claims to be the perfect explanation for everything. But according to Buddha human consciousness is the highest form of consciousness in the universe. Hence we realise that our new understanding of the nature of the universe of which the methods and enquiries of the new sciences have become the accepted means of information are helping us to realise that the state of religious explanations for the creation and preservation of all life is drawing to a close. We are truly grown up adults now. I find this new acknowledgement of the nature of things wholly satisfying and I am thankful to have got there. I also think that the fact that fewer people go to church these days is a positive sign of their having grown up and being able to take more responsibility for their own lives rather than having lost their faith."

EG and, he suspects, many other people in the pews have taken a not dissimilar, if less explicit view of religious commitment for some time, without pursuing it to its logical conclusion. They adopt the autonomy model of divine intervention altogether. So perhaps their current attitude to faith is not far from Rosemarie's model of the supercession of belief after all.

Nothing has so far come of EG's concern for asylum seekers because his health took a turn for the worse during the year. A scan showed him to have suffered a series of mini-strokes which required a quieter life-style all round. This has now been implemented with lengthy rests after a morning's work and a much-reduced amount of time in London and/or at meetings. That has also involved much reduced participation in community life. So we are glad to have Ena Dilley three mornings a week to deal with the administrative chores, and Francis McGrory as a working housekeeper. Without them the household would not run so well.

Having Martin in Leeds just along the M62 and Philip and Frieda in their house in Northenden on the other side of the Mersey (when they are not in Zambia) puts us in close touch with each other. Philip feels that his time in charge of the Kaloko Trust is probably coming to an end since he will have done fifteen years in Zambia in the New Year.

Janet in Hong Kong is also inclined to think that her time there is coming to an end. So it may be that she and Martin will move to a house in the neighbourhood of Leeds in the course of the year. That would bring most of the family into the Manchester-Leeds axis.

Crispin's health has much improved. He is in control of his life and makes splendid music with his musical friends. He is also an attender at the Quakers' meetings in town. Twice a week he helps the Oxfam shop in the village to press their second hand clothes. On the whole he prefers these freelance activities to a single full-time job.

Becca and her friend Shulamit have been hoping to have a baby by intra-vitro fertilisation. In Becca's case she turned out to be too old. Shulamit has just had a little girl, whom we shall of course, welcome into our family circle. These non-marital additions to the family require a new nomenclature and description. We are experimenting with this, and will no doubt come up with the appropriate phrase. This is more urgent since EG has been editing a more or less complete genealogy of his great-grandparents who had fifteen children, thirteen of whom survived into adulthood.

Tom appears to be settling in well at Eastbourne College. Besides his prowess at Rugger - he has been scoring for the under fifteen team - he has been following in his chemical great-grandfather's footsteps academically and continues in his artistic endeavours.

The 2004 letter

THIS LETTER APPEARS to be largely concerned with our family affairs; Martin at Leeds University, Philip retiring from the Kaloko Trust, and the letter includes the retirement of the Kaloko Founder. We also comment on the increasing trend for young families to break up.

18 Cranmer Road
Manchester
M20 0AW

Advent 2004

Now that we are well launched into the new century, and getting used to referring to the 20th century as in the past, we are able to regard old age as a new period of life, in all likelihood the terminal one. We have already outlived many of our contemporaries, many of those who remain are too frail to move easily. Since our move from London to Manchester we have always regarded ourselves as relatively peripatetic. By means of the Chantry Group which has met twice a year we have kept in touch.

The family is more in touch than in the past. Martin is well settled in Leeds as the Director of the Overseas Relations of the Faculty of Education there. He is just back from China and South Korea where he pursues the international interests of the Faculty. Janet, his wife has retired from her work in Hong Kong. They are now exploring how life together works out when lived in the same place

Philip, having retired from the directorship of the Kaloko Trust (see *Kaloko News* attached) has decided to work in the private sector. At present he lives in Northenden and Frieda works in a BUPA old peoples' home. The better food and the more settled conditions of life have resulted in an unexpected addition to the family, Philip and Frieda expect a baby next May. In the meantime Tom now plays for the second Rugger team as Eastbourne

45. With our French neighbours at Vigneau, 1987.

46. Vigneau June 1994: Martin, Philip, Rebecca and Crispin.

47. Vigneau: Olga Pocock Renate and Sophia, EGW and Rosemarie, 2009.

48. Dinner at Vigneau September 2010: Sophia, EGW, Rosemarie and Martin.

49. Rosemarie in the pool at Vigneau.

50. Bowles at Vigneau Summer 1985.

51. *Lunch at Vigneau with Ian Gilbert, James Mark, Jeremy Rose and Crispin.*

College as he prepares for the GCSE.

We have had another addition to the family. As forecast last year, in the arrival of Chanya, by now a determined one-year old who certainly keeps her two "Mothers" Rebecca and Shulamit busy. Since they are both working full-time they wonder how we coped with four offspring when we were young! Since the autumn Becca has been a half-time lecturer in Singing at Havering College of Further Education, a welcome addition to her workload.

Crispin has become more closely linked with the Manchester Friends at their Meeting House in Mount Street. The Clozapine treatment involves monthly blood tests and a fairly rigorous regime of medication. But the return of his capacity for self-management has been remarkable. He now runs an active life without significant supervision. His contribution to Oxfam, the Liberal Democrat cause and the Quaker connection alongside his musical career is something we would not at one time have thought possible.

In the wider family we have experienced the strains and stresses under which the young families live their lives. It is evident that many marriages are no longer for life, and that our nephews and nieces more often change partners at or around midlife. We suppose that is one of the changes in lifestyle which are now more marked between the initial enthusiasm with which the young enter into a commitment, and the changing opportunities of middle life. We try to maintain relationships with both sides of a broken marriage without losing track of what we regard as a life-long commitment. That requires a fair ability to deal with changing circumstances without making judgements. On occasion we need to provide support, both moral and practical, to families in trouble.

The passage of time is also depriving us of our well-established landmarks in the family. Klaus Meyer whose ninetieth birthday we celebrated by a river trip last summer, died earlier this year. A family tree of the fifteen children of Samuel Meyer of Hanover which we produced for his birthday has enabled us to link some of those belonging to that remarkable branch of our family. The death of Harold Lockley also removed the senior member of another branch of the family this year, bereaving the children of EG's Sister Ursula of their remaining link to the older generation.

We were glad to strengthen the links with Klaus and Nina's two children, both of whom with their families spent holidays at Vigneau. It seems possible that some of our American cousins will also spend holidays there in the near future. All this shows that for Rosemarie and me the horizon has shifted. But perhaps that is no bad thing, bearing in mind that all families need to reflect on their own raison d'être from time to time. The death of Rosemarie's Sister

Inge, who was a much loved family aunt, added to our sorrows. She had been crippled with arthritis and life had become to be burden for her. Her care for her nephews and nieces was exemplary, and they remember her with much affection.

Even with these family concerns wider issues have occupied EG during the year. The first is the approaching fiftieth anniversary of the death of George Bell, our much loved Bishop of Chichester. The excellent biography by Ronald Jasper published in 1967 covered the wide range of Bell's interests both within the Church of England and beyond. But material has become available since then, about Bell's involvement in the ecumenical movement of the Churches, and in maintenance of his role in the efforts of the German resistance which may lead to a reassessment of his contribution. EG hopes to write a short piece about the significance of Bell's work during and after the war.

The other arises from a visit which Philip and EG made to the concentration camp at Flossenburg, where Dietrich Bonhoeffer was murdered in 1945. Material collected by the Faculty of Law of the University of Amsterdam is a separate footnote to the biography of Bonhoeffer, which we hope will appear in *Humanitas*, the journal of the George Bell Institute.

Rosemarie writes:

> Having read through last year's letter I feel that I have nothing to add to what I said then. I am thankful to affirm day by day, my closeness to nature in its manifold manifestations of living organisms and creatures. As a family we have much reason to give thanks for health and strength, and real friendship. We are lucky to meet our friends through the Chantry Group and in other ways.

The 2005 letter

ROSEMARIE had a late developing enthusiasm for History. As a birth-right historian EG was delighted. The publication of *A Memoir of Troubled Times* recalled the status of asylum seekers of the family back in 1939. Migration seems to be nothing new. We also began periods in hospital that year.

18 Cranmer Road
Manchester
M20 0AW

1st Sunday in Advent 27/11/05

Rosemarie has for many years been a writer of travel diaries. There is now quite a pile of these written during her travels to Philip, in India and Zambia and to Martin, in China and elsewhere. We think it may be worthwhile publishing these, so that is what we are doing at the present and we hope they will be out in time for next Christmas.

Rosemarie writes

Last year I wrote that I have 'outgrown religion'. I confirm that this year and add that the study of history and science have, for me, replaced it. History is as, if not more, important than science to help us understand how and why our own religion has evolved from the beginnings in Palestine. The fact that both St John and St Paul lived and wrote their letters from Tarsus and Ephesus respectively, cities in modern Turkey, then being part of the Greco - Roman empire, confirms my belief in the importance of the historical background of the events which have created and shaped the religion of believers living in the former Greco - Roman empire. Increasingly, I find the study of history most rewarding. I believe that the effect of marginalising it has had serious consequences, and will continue to have, if we go on thinking that it is not that important.

Another publishing venture is an English edition of Vom Segen des Glaubens, which most of you will not have seen. It was published in German by the Church of the Rhineland about ten years ago as a memoir of EG's parents. It deals with the troubled years when the Nazis tried to destroy the family, together with millions of other families living generally godly and quiet lives. The enormity of the undertaking takes the breath away, even at this distance in time. But for the efforts of conscientious people, such as George Bell, the Bishop of Chichester, the Nazis would have succeeded.

EG remembers his father saying that he would not, indeed could not, think of emigrating away from his own country, but in the end that is what he had to do. My mother bore the brunt of moving their family of four children, and she was fortunate in having support in this country. It was only the devoted help of our friends that saved us.

We think it is worthwhile to tell the tale, if only as an example of one ordinary family of asylum seekers, of whom today there seems to be an unending stream. What has changed in seventy years? Globalisation seems to be the main factor, changing both the scale and the nature of the quest for asylum. In the event, the Pilgrim fathers, the Huguenots, the Protestants of Salzburg and the Germans from Silesia, show that migration is nothing new. The variable is the amount of duress exercised. On the whole our family was able to weather the storm. The rest, as they say, is history.

Martin and Janet, now back from Hong Kong, are about to move into an old farmhouse on the edge of Leeds, which they intend to renovate. Cris has a new clarinet tutor and continues the chamber concerts with David Morgan. They recently raised about £200 for the Arab-Israeli community at Neve Shalom. It looks as though these types of initiative may have more of a future than we ever thought if Mr Sharon manages to break the political impasse. Phil has bought a dog and cat boarding kennel with a business partner who was involved in the support of the Koloko Trust. Glebe Farm, just south of the Humber in Yorkshire, is a pleasant and well found enterprise. Phil and Frieda's move from largely benefit orientated activities to a commercial enterprise raised eyebrows here. But we think it is quite understandable when seen in the context of Phil's twenty-two years of life abroad as a volunteer. The arrival of Emily as Thomas' stepsister has made us all very happy. She and Tom have struck up an instant rapport. Chanya, Becca and Shulamit's two year old, is a bundle of energy who wears out both her mothers! Rosemarie looks forward to having Emily and Chanya together at Vigneau, when they will no doubt make the most of the garden and the pool. The house down there is getting a lot of use, about which we are very glad. We ourselves had two months there in April and September.

Rosemarie and EG both had time in hospital in July-August, so that we missed the Schubertiade in Austria. We now take life very quietly with plenty of rest.

The 2006 letter

THE PUBLICATION OF *Halfway Round the World* about Rosemarie's travels was quickly sold out following her book signing party in Didsbury village. This was also the year when Jacques Delors retired from the Presidency of the European Commission. He had been instrumental in launching the "Soul for Europe" initiative, which found a strong support from European religious communities. The quarrel between those who think religion is relevant and important and those who don't ended in the victory of the latter. That was sad.

18 Cranmer Road
Manchester
M20 0AW

2nd Sunday in Advent 2006

We have survived another year. In spite of two spells in hospital EG is no worse in the cardiac department than at the beginning of the year, although the pace of his life has slowed down and the intake of pills has increased.

The book of Rosemarie's diaries of her travels in China, India and Central Africa came out in September. The Memoir Club did a good job with a paperback edition. We were able to hold a book signing of *Halfway Round the World* in David Rushton's shop along the road. The first printing has been taken up and a second edition is almost exhausted.

The other manuscript we mentioned last year has been rather slower off the mark, but is now well on the way. The English title will be *A Memoir of troubled Times* and it will be published by New European Publications, John Coleman's firm. Maggie Hoeffgen of the German Department of the University and the Goethe Institute has translated those parts which our Niece Katherine Wedell had not been able to deal with. We think it is worth publishing the story because the thirties, forties and fifties of the last century were indeed troubled times, of much consequence for this family.

Broadcasting at the Crossroads published by McMillans, has had a belated flowering since the changes which Bryan Luckham and I had foreseen at the time are now coming about. The resignation of Michael Grade from the chairmanship of the BBC in order to become executive chairman of what remains of ITV illustrates our point. The broadcasting arena has been reduced to a two horse race: public policy is irrelevant.

The European scene is puzzling. On the one hand the actual integration is proceeding at a rate of knots. One can and does go anywhere; jobs are available wherever one wants to go; and we are almost back to the days before passports were invented. On the other hand, the actual EU management structure creaks and seems to suffer from bureaucratic overkill. We have been hearing about the fate of the Soul for Europe initiative, taken by Jacques Delors and virtually killed off after his departure. It may be that the project was one step too far, and that the "democratic" procedures, which we use to settle EU affairs are not capable of dealing with the more subtle matters of belief and conviction. Do we then devise alternative procedures or do we abandon the attempt to tackle them?

This also raises the related issue of institutional identification. The Roman Catholic institutions, for example, can take positions which are clearly defined one way or another. Less centralised bodies of opinion may be just as important, but may lack cohesive organs for the articulation of their views. So there is a tendency for the more obvious and easily defined positions to get more attention than those that are less defined. We need to discover means of achieving consensus or the means of agreeing to differ, in the more elusive areas of judgement.

Tom is doing A levels in the new year and, on present form, is due to find something useful to do at university. Quite what that will he remains to be identified. The second generation of grandchildren. Philip & Frieda's Emily, and Shulamit and Becca's Chanya, are learning to walk and talk. We are delighted to watch them doing that. Martin and Janet's house is proving very satisfactory. Janet is currently doing a locum in Hong King, but apart from that devoting herself to interior decorating. Crispin is engrossed in variations of musical performance, both as soloist and in ensembles. Next Saturday, David Sandiford is paying a Lord Mayor's visitation to Cris' concert in support of the Kaloko Trust.

The 2007 letter

THE NATURE OF LIBERAL VALUES in the European political scene came to our notice through out participation in the Liberal Democrat Congress in Berlin. We were told that liberal values in the parliamentary systems in Europe and the rest of the world were largely lacking. We maintain that liberal values are vital on the global scales, and worth struggling for. On the domestic front, it was interesting to see the success of Philip's natural sympathy with dogs in the support for his kennels. Tom's decision to go to Manchester University rather than try his luck at Oxford's Mansfield College was in the family tradition.

18 Cranmer Road
Manchester
M20 0AW

2nd Sunday in Advent 2007

We hope our Christmas Greetings will reach you in time. We are on the whole in good fettle and hope to live to complete our sixtieth year of married life on 5th April 2008. We would be delighted if those of you who can would join us on 31st May, when we hope to mark the event with a lunch and some music. We shall do so at the University's Chancellor's House in Fallowfield.

EG has given up trying to follow the fortunes of what used to be a television system which he could understand The sheer range and technical diversity is now such that full-time attention is required if one is to master it.

We are more concerned with the way the country is being run. We are glad about the convergence of mainstream political opinion around the centre ground. We would like that to be reflected in the political structures. But these are out-of-date. The parties are reluctant to venture out of their habitual stances and resist change. It was ever thus. Rosemarie and I went as make-weights with the British Delegation to the European Liberal Democrat

Congress in Berlin in October. The guests from Vietnam, Georgia and the West Bank pointed out that the Europeans enjoy the representation of liberal values in their parliamentary systems; something lacking in many parts of the world. That reminder served to lift us out of our petty concern with local politicking. Liberal values are vital on a global scale, and worth struggling for.

Turning to family matters, Crispin is more and more involved in musical activities. In addition to the Music-for-Pleasure choir of Roger Wilkes he has now joined the Cavendish Singers. He has formed a Wind Trio and joined the Manchester Music Makers. At a more academic level he will be staring an Open University Music Course in February.

Martin flies around the world in the educational interests of Leeds University, having been in Chile in the summer, he is now just back from strengthening the link with China. His new book on educational management came out in September. He is negotiating a reduction of time with the University, so as to be less pressed. He and Janet are comfortable in the new house. Janet spent two months helping out in her old college in Hong Kong.

Philip and Frieda's Emily keeps them both on their toes. Philip's kennels appear to be doing well. The local people like to bring their dogs largely, we are told, because they are well treated and taken for walks. Becca's musical activities flourish alongside her preoccupation with Chanya, who is a very lively four year old. She seems to exhaust both Shulamit and Becca in equal measure to their delight. Tom, now an 18 year old school leaver, is at present in Australia for his gap year. He had three A's in the summer and is determined to go to Manchester, who have offered him a place next year, rather than try his luck at Mansfield College, Oxford. *De gustibus non disputandum*, as they say.

The 2008 letter

THE ENGLISH TEXT of *A Memoir of Troubled Times* was kindly reviewed by Tim Lee:

> Gertride's astute and sensitive diaries illustrate well the power of faith to sustain through troubled and less troubled times.

Certainly the story which is now passing out of the consciousness of the generation which lived through these times is noteworthy. We celebrated our sixtieth wedding anniversary, which these day is rare. The children organised a splendid lunch party for which Rosemarie and I were very grateful. The fiftieth anniversary of the death of George Bell, the Bishop of Chichester, was the reason for recalling his courageous and generous care of the "non-Aryan" Christians in Germany. I suppose that was the single most significant reaction of the Church to the politics of another country.

18 Cranmer Road
Manchester
M20 0AW

2nd Sunday in Advent 2008

Christmas is here again and we try to encapsulate twelve months of life into a single page of greetings.

An important event of the year was the publication in English, twelve years after its original publication in German, of the account of Hans and Gertrude's experiences in the 1930's and 1940's. John Coleman, editor of the New European Publications took great trouble with the manuscript and produced it under the title *A Memoir of Troubled Times*. In spite of the story being about events long passed Tim Lee's review in *Together* found it relevant. He called it a love story "Gertrude's astute and sensitive diaries illustrate well the power of faith to sustain through troubled and less troubled times."

We were glad to be able to publish the book on the day of our sixtieth wedding anniversary at the end of May. Martin and Janet, Crispin, Philip and Freda and Rebecca and Shulamit gave us a splendid lunch. So many of our friends and relations turned out that Chancellor's House had to add a marquee onto the dining room to get them all in. It was a lovely day and we were most grateful.

EG felt that he should mark the fiftieth anniversary of the death of George Bell, Bishop of Chichester, by recalling the Bishop's courageous care of the so called Non-Aryan Christians in a brief paper. It is not generally known that in November 1938 he single-handedly guaranteed to the Home Office the support of twenty German pastors and their families who were persecuted by the Nazis following the "Kristallnacht" progroms in 1938. That enabled the Home Office to give them entry visas. In this way the Wedells were rescued, and the rest is history. *The Church Times* reprinted the relevant parts of EG's paper which was also published in *Humanitas* the journal of the George Bell Institute.

As ever, there is a steady demand from people who like to come to Vigneau for their holidays. We have developed two streams: one of friends who can afford to pay the market rate, and another of those who cannot, but who obviously benefit from their time in the house and garden and pool. By putting the two alongside each other we are able to maintain it at a proper level. We have a month down there ourselves in the spring and autumn. Being 10 degrees further south than Manchester makes a noticeable difference to the climate and the weather.

Our second generation of grandchildren give us much joy. Chanya is now at school, Emily is eighteen months younger, and Lina is flourishing at six months.

The 2009 letter

THIS WAS THE beginning of the Lib Dem - Conservative Coalition. Before the election, I had counselled my local party to link up with the Labour Party. Since the arithmetic was against that a coalition with the Conservatives was worth considering. It was, in retrospect, a wise decision which will have long term consequences for the nature of politics in the country. We hope that the age of the Conservative/Labour ding-dong is at long last over. The enthusiasm of British expatriates for the Anglican tradition represented in south west France is interesting. All sorts and conditions of Christians and sceptics gather to support the Anglican First Cause. It is certainly more successful than the Roman Catholic one in this area. Martin's writing on Educational Planning is receiving a lot of praise; we are very glad.

18 Cranmer Road
Manchester
M20 0AW

Advent 2009

We look forward to Christmas and hope that it will be a time of blessing for you and your families.

The weeks of Advent have always had a strong air of expectancy in our family. The annual rehearsal of the arrival of the Christ-child into our world of strife and disaster is a reminder of the hope of a new beginning which persists however decrepit we become.

This last year we have been concerned with three problems close to us, even though we are by now distant from any active involvement in them. The most worrying is the extent to which the machinery of government appears to be incapable of solving our political problems. There is little doubt that we need a moderate left-of-centre administration, and that a Lib Dem-Labour coalition would ensure that. But the animosity of the two parties at local level renders a sensible compromise unlikely. One wishes there might be an alternative on the right of centre, but the hopelessly anti-European pressures on the Conservative right seem to rule out any chance of that happening. So the political options seem to be bleak.

The failure of nerve in Anglican circles is our second concern, even though EG, Philip and Emily are currently the only active supporters of the established Church. Martin has been to a Western Buddhist retreat in Wales, Crispin is an intermittent supporter of the Friends' Meeting in town, and Becca's compositions reinforce the musical quality of the reformed Judaism promoted by Shulamit. Rosemarie's long pilgrimage has currently led her to abandon God; and we pray that God will not give up on her.

We see the strength of the popular support for the Anglican tradition both at St Paul's in Withington, and at the lovely 13th Century church at Monteton, about 10 minutes from Vigneau. There the virtual demise of the Roman Catholic diocese is replaced by a larger and vigorous expatriate congregation of Anglicans, ministered to by a Dutch Chaplain who became an Anglican in Singapore. EG is certain that the continuing strength of the Church of England was not lost on the Pope during his recent meeting with Rowan Williams. The bankruptcy of Roman Catholic leadership in Ireland, the USA and elsewhere cannot be camouflaged by diversionary tactics devised by the Roman Curia.

EG has recently been revisiting the memorandum he wrote about the tasks and organisation of the (then new) Board of Social Responsibility when he was the Secretary in 1960. It has survived fifty years rather well even though its successor is now called the Mission and Public Affairs Division.

Lastly, the management of the University is quite unable to ensure the regular tutorial support of Undergraduates. Our vice-Chancellor (now designated President) wrings his hands in the University journal, but seems unable to secure enough competent staff to deal with the absurdly inflated student numbers. Our Grandson Tom came here because of the family connection, but finds support hard to find. Most of the money seems to be going on the President's ambitions for globally-significant research, leaving the University without the means to realise its responsibilities as one of the major civic universities in the country. Martin reports similar folies-de-grandeur from Leeds when he touches base there in the course of his global tours of China, India and South America. He new book on *Planning for Education Change* is reaping rave reviews.

Our grandchildren are growing up fast. Chanya and Emily are now at school, both bringing home school reports which make their parents blush.

We hope that they will survive in an educational maelstrom which has become hopelessly complicated since EG had to do with it. Lina is as yet uncontaminated by outside issues: long may she remain so.

The 2010 letter

ROSEMARIE DIED ON September 14th after we and our friends had dinner at the Vieux Porche; a good way to die. So we had no Christmas letter that year. Instead, we circulated the text of her funeral and her memorial service in Manchester.

Rosemarie's Life

She was one of the group of intrepid women who, in the middle of the last war, prepared themselves to help the churches in war-torn Europe to rebuild their lives at the end of the conflict. Having come to this country in 1939 to improve her English, she decided on the outbreak of hostilities to stay here. In the event, Rosemarie was appointed after her training to the parish of Holzhausen in Westphalia, where her father was then the vicar. She used her acquired skills to rebuild the work for young people in the parish, which had been prohibited during the Nazi years.

In 1948 she returned to England and was asked by the YWCA to launch a Youth Club in Chorlton-on-Medlock, which at that time was one of the most deprived areas of Manchester. She worked intensively with young people who had never had anyone to take an interest in them. Her willingness to go the extra mile to realise their potential was the hallmark of her work in those years.

In 1964 Rosemarie was appointed as religious education specialist in two of the toughest secondary schools. She was also appointed a Justice of the Peace, but she was not willing to sit in judgement on people, many of whom she thought were more sinned against than sinning. So she resigned her commission and concentrated on the personal work in the classroom.

In the 1970's Rosemarie was put in charge of the English speaking religious education in the European School. Her interest in the inter-faith character of her work in schools led her to develop her work in that direction.

In 1980 she became a founder member of the Board of the Faculty for the Comparative Study of Religions at the Vrije Universiteit of Brussels. Later; she spent several years travelling in India, China and Africa to refine her understanding of the major world faiths. Her experiences and insights were set out in *Halfway Round the World* which was published in 2006.

On her return Rosemarie taught comparative religion in the Manchester College of Adult Education and in the University of the Third Age.

Her death and the funeral service on 17/9/2010

Rosemarie was frail but enjoyed the lovely weather and the views over the fields and woods beyond our garden.

Towards lunchtime on the 14th her heart gave out. She wanted to be cremated and for her ashes to be scattered at Vigneau and the rose garden at Cranmer Road. So her funeral service was held at Tonneins and conducted by Revd Dr Paul Vrolijk, the Anglican Chaplain.

After his words of welcome, I explained that Rosemarie was my wife for over sixty-two years. We shared by far the major parts of our lives. She was born in Westphalia. By choice she became a British citizen. Her vocation was to be a citizen of Europe.

All her life she worked to discover the truth;
- the truth about the meaning of our existence
- the truth about our European, indeed our global future;
- the truth about the many faiths of India;
- the truth about a lively agricultural and social life in Africa which
  Philip was developing;
- the truth about the future of China where Martin was working
- the truth about religion which the World Congress of Faiths is seeking.

Today we celebrate with her the achievement of her life's search: God has revealed to her the knowledge of the truth: Hallelujah!

Rev Dr Ann Shukman who was at Vigneau with other members of the Chantry Group read a passage from the book about Nicholas Berdyaev's Philosophy of Personalism* which Rosemarie had on her bedside table.

"Man is a spiritual being, the child of the eternal, and as such pertains to an order which is timeless... the spirit of man contains within it all the properties, potentialities and attributes of the divine... the soul which is open to the invasion of the spirit thus experiences an extension of its personality, inter penetrating and inter penetrated by the personalities of its fellows; this is the natural activity of the spirit, and is called love".

*Nicolas Berdyaev by George Seaver, London. James Clarke 1950 Pages 20-23
Then we sang *The Pilgrim's Song* by John Bunyan (1684) and Others.

Crispin played **Après un rêve by G. Fauré** accompanied by Janie Tervet.

Martin said:

> By birth Rosemarie was a country girl.. it showed.. she loved being outside, in the sun.. under the moon.. she loved the fruit-picking she did as rent for Starvecrow when we were children, and for the second half of her life she loved the trees and flowers in her Manchester garden. She passed that love of nature on.
>
> She was a woman with quite simple material needs and desires. Her 'waste not want not' approach to life was bit of a family joke. Now I'm grateful for the model. Daily life CAN be simple.
>
> She was always a European/world citizen, never a nationalist. She was interested in ideas of all kinds and people from all places. She understood how interdependent we are as inhabitants of a single world and so the need for openness to each other's cultures and ideas. She was a lifelong learner and encouraged us to be likewise.
>
> To be a lifelong learner she had to remain open-minded. And in many ways she succeeded in being so. On her journey through life she was never afraid to move on in her thinking, even when it meant discarding some of the apparent certainties of the moment. In this intellectual sense she was a brave woman, and has set me quite a challenge.
>
> Ultimately of course she was an ordinary person, she was my mother, and I shall miss her.

Rebecca said:

> Where do people go when they die?

This is the question my young daughter asked on hearing that her grandma had died. We tell her that our bodies return to the earth, and we tell her that all that grandma has been will continue in the hearts and minds of everyone whose lives she has touched.

For 30 years my mother spent her summers on the Spanish coast near Alicante. There she contemplated the moon in its journey across the sky, and the ever-changing motions and colours of the sea. It became, over the years, a part of her spiritual meditation, deepening in these last years as she looked out on the gardens at Vigneau, in France, and at home in Manchester.

So, in the rising of the sun and its going down, we may remember her. In the blowing of the wind and in the chill of winter, we may remember her. In the rustling of the leaves and in the beauty of autumn, we may remember her. As long as we live, so too shall she live for she is now a part of us, as we remember her.'

In these final couple of years she suffered physically and mentally. Now, we can tell my daughter, grandma is at rest.

This evening is the beginning of the Jewish festival of Yom Kippur, the Day of Atonement. It is a time of self-reflection and remembrance of our loved ones.

This funeral prayer, EI Maleh Rachmim is traditionally sung at this time:

> O God, full of compassion, grant perfect rest under the wings of your presence, to the soul of Rosemarie who has gone to her eternal home. Merciful God, remember her merits and the righteous deeds which she performed on earth. Open for her the gates of righteousness and light, of compassion and grace. Shelter her for ever under your loving care and let her soul be bound up in the gathering of life.

May she rest in peace, and let us say 'Amen'

Paul Vrolijk repeated John 14 and said:

> In my Father's house are many rooms.

As I was thinking about these words yesterday evening, I had to think about Vigneau as a foretaste of heaven. Vigneau of course the place where Rosemarie and George and the family spent many happy times together. Vigneau has many rooms... perfect for hide-and-seek as my children and nieces told me! A place with many rooms. A place of warmth and welcome. A place of generous hospitality! And at the heart of the house a long dining table... where people dine, talk and enjoy French cooking. A foretaste of the heavenly banquet? I met Rosemarie on two occasions at Vigneau over a meal. What struck me was her kindness. Especially to my children! Vigneau... a place of warmth, love, hospitality.

When Jesus spoke of his Father's house as a place of eternal welcome, his disciples did not have a clue what he was talking about. There might be several people here who have such questions or doubts. That's why it is wonderful that finding the way to that house of many rooms does not depend on us knowing everything... or being perfect people... but on trust... belief, we can have in a person... Jesus Christ. As Jesus said:

> Let not your hearts be troubled. Believe in God; believe also in me.

At the start of the service we sang "He (or better she!) who would valiant be... to be a pilgrim." Although we are all on a journey, we are not meant to remain 'pilgrims' forever. Our destiny is to come home... to find our destiny in that house of many rooms... I find it of real comfort that Jesus elsewhere in the gospels promises us that those who 'go on seeking' will find... and that those who 'go on knocking' that door will be opened for them. The door to that house of many rooms... that place of eternal warmth and welcome.

After the Lords prayer we sang **À toi la gloire, O Ressuscité**! A hymn which Rosemarie and I first sang at the Assembly of the World Council of Churches in Amsterdam in 1948.

Finally, Paul Vrolijk pronounced the Committal and the Blessing.

Her Memorial on 28/11/10

Since Rosemarie's funeral had taken place in France we decided to hold a gathering to remember her life in Manchester. This took place on Advent Sunday 2010 at Chancellor's House of the University of Manchester. A large number of Rosemarie's relations and friends travelled from all parts of the country and Belgium and Germany to join the 150 or more participants in the gathering.

At its opening the **Revd. Gisela Raynes**, rector of our parish church of St Paul in Withington, read:

Kindness
By Naomi Shihab Nye

Before you know what kindness really is
you must lose things,
feel the future dissolve in a moment like
salt in a weakened broth.
What you held in your hand,
what you counted and carefully saved,
all this must go so you know
how desolate the landscape can be
between the regions of kindness.
How you ride. and ride
thinking the bus will never stop;
the passengers eating maize and chicken
will stare out the window forever.

Before you learn the tender gravity of
kindness, you must travel where the
Indian in a white poncho
lies dead by the side of the road.
You must see how this could be you,
how he too was someone
who journeyed though the night with
plans

and the simple breath that kept
him alive

Before you know kindness as the
deepest thing inside,
you must know sorrow as the
other deepest thing.
You must wake up with sorrow.
You must speak to it till your voice
catches the thread of all sorrows
and you see the size of the cloth.

Then it is only kindness that makes
sense anymore,
only kindness that ties your shoes
and sends you out into the day to
mail letters and purchase bread,
only kindness that raises its head
from the crowd of the world to say
it is I you have been looking for,
and then goes with you every where
like a shadow or a friend.

There followed contributions from Rosemarie's friends:

Rosemarie and the Young

Satima Witts (a former Buddhist nun and now a mother of two boys)

Being my god-mother, I really did feel that she took that role to heart.
She was caring, constant guardian, who was there at important moments in my life. She visited when I was a Buddhist nun and discussed the spiritual life and women's place in it, with me. She had a great understanding of Buddhist practice and obviously practised a reflective and compassionate approach to life.
She was great at staying in touch and always remembered each Christmas and every birthday. She phoned just after having returned from Vigneau one year and explained that she was becoming ever more frail and her memory was going somewhat. I felt that she was almost saying 'goodbye' already, and had the kindness and compassion to let me know this.
I really do feel that her caring and compassionate energy is very much here today, and that the passing of the body, allows the beauty of heart to shine even more.

Elisabeth Wright (a lifelong friend)

I have known Rosemarie since I was four years old. She studied Theology at Wistow Training centre, where my parents were also students and part of the leadership team - as was "Mumchen", Eberhard's mother. Rosemarie was training during the war to become a Parish Worker in post-war Germany. Every morning during this time Rosemarie and I would come skipping down the Wistow Hall's grand staircase, singing, "Here we come skipping down the stairs ...early in the morning." This memory was to stay with Rosemarie for the rest of her life - at least she referred to it every time I subsequently met her. Even Eberhard quoted it to me recently on the phone.
In retrospect, I have become very aware of what that action says about Rosemarie - her patience, her understanding, her empathy, her kindness, her generosity towards a youngster like me - and therefore I assume to all around her.
I also well remember my mother often quoting how Rosemarie had said to her that she was going to wait for Eberhard. Theirs was one of the first Wistow marriages, and I was privileged to be one of the flower girls at their wedding in 1948.
We kept in touch during subsequent years.
I remember visiting Rosemarie and Eberhard for a weekend during my early teaching years. I felt able to discuss my personal problems with Rosemarie and felt uncritically understood and accepted.
A few years ago, I again visited Rosemarie and Eberhard for a few days. I was so pleased to experience Rosemarie in her own rooms and to feel her affection and warmth and her interest in us as a family. On that occasion I remember asking her about some "churchy" issue that was disturbing me at that time, to

which she replied something like that she had outgrown the church. Although I might not have used that formulation, I feel we shared very similar views on most religious and social issues.

Rosemarie has in many ways accompanied me throughout my life and I have been most grateful for her helpful and sound advice as well as her friendship and understanding. She has my most sincere admiration. I feel so very grateful to her.

Barbara Grant Pearce (a former pupil)

In 1968 I was fourteen and, art not being my strongest subject, I was staring vacantly from the classroom window. A car pulled up and parked in the driveway. When the attractive lady driver came over to ask me to point her in the direction of the school office, I was looking down into Rosemarie's brown eyes. Little did I know that this was the start of a loving friendship that would last more than forty years.

Rosemarie came to St Margaret's Secondary School to teach us RE. We learned about Judaism, Islam, Buddhism and, of course, Christianity. For our course work we also undertook practical projects that informed us about provisions for the disabled and other social facilities. We even visited elderly citizens to assist them in their homes. But our favourite subject was the social discussions we had with Rosemarie on Friday afternoons - possibly between maths and music - when the topics covered ranged from what we could do as humane young people to help the victims of the Biafran war, to the desperate physical needs... of men.

Always open and candid about everything, Rosemarie allowed us a peek through a door and into an area about which, naturally, we were consumed by curiosity. Rosemarie gave free rein to our imagination and answered every feverish question honestly and openly. How our young minds danced with delight as we pictured candle-lit dinners on balmy evenings and romantic, moonlit meanderings on beaches with handsome boyfriends... Boy-_what_? This was the point where our breathtaking reveries were shattered by the image of our stern, protective parents.

And at the end of these sessions we would say wistfully to one another, 'I wish my mum was like Mrs Wedell.' Rosemarie was at least one generation ahead of her time!

Years later, Rosemarie would contact me and together, as two women, we would attend meetings at the Teachers' Centre and other venues to listen to writers and educationalists sharing their ideas. After an absence of nearly ten years in Nigeria, one of the first places I visited on my return to the UK was Cranmer Road and, of course, Rosemarie was still here and still busy organising a number of events, including glorious musical evenings, to raise money for the charities which characterised her giving and generous nature.

These are just a few of the many thoughtful things that Rosemarie did. I feel extremely honoured to have known this amazing woman, to have been admitted into the heart of her home, to have enjoyed so much hospitality and to have shared events that meant so much to her. I know Rosemary is in a place where only the kindest, sweetest spirits rest; and my deepest heartfelt wish is that this is not goodbye but *auf wiedersehen.*

Dr Feng Dong (who lived with her family in the Wedell house in Cranmer Road)

Mrs. Rosemarie Wedell is very friendly to us all. I remembered when we first arrived Manchester in 1993, she introduced friends to us to avoid we feel lonely. I can still remember the family concert, lovely tea parties.

When I had my PhD viva, she let me stay with her on the night before the viva. In that evening, she and Crispin played card games with me to comfort my nerves. How considerate she is.

Once I visited the Whitworth Art Gallery, surprisingly found a carpet that looked familiar. When I looked the details, find out that was the Persian carpet in Rosemarie's sitting room, she donated to the Art Gallery.

She is nice to her friends and she is also committed to her work. When she was working in adult education college, she taught a part of Chinese history. She specially made a trip with Jeremy's mother to visit to our students' accommodation. At the tea party, she asks our opinion about that period. How devoted to the job she was, which impressed me.

Reading her book *Halfway around the World*, I can see that she is generous to many people she met and give her love to almost everybody. That is why she can make so many friends internationally.

We are in great sorrow with you, miss her greatly, without Rosemarie, Manchester is different. I will always remember her. Rosemarie's kind, nice, optimist, active and lovely image will always live in our heart. She gave her love to people and people loved her. She will be missed by all of us.

Rosemarie and Education

Roger Wilkes (a colleague at the College of Adult Education)

It was very kind of George to invite me to say, now, a few words about Rosemarie, with particular reference to her involvement with the former College of Adult Education in Manchester where we both worked. This is something which I now do with pleasure, even though my specific relevant knowledge is limited.

I'll come to the College itself in a moment, but, before that, I'd like to refer to two sources which I've found helpful in assembling my comments: (i) the observation in the Times Obituary dated 1 November, that Rosemarie was much influenced by the Sea of Faith movement launched by Don Cupitt", and (ii) by remarks attributed to Martin at Rosemarie's Funeral Service in France on 17 September. The Revd. Don Cupitt, for any of you who have not come across him before, is a Life Fellow of Emmanuel College, Cambridge, where he was a Fellow between 1965 and 1996, Dean from 1966 to 1991, and University Lecturer in Divinity from 1973 til 1996. Incidentally, before he held any of those positions, he was Curate at St Philip's Church, Salford, from 1959 to 1962, so there is a local connection. Cupitt's extensive list of publications includes many which venture beyond sectarian Christianity, and *The Sea of Faith* of

1984, especially given its association with a BBC television series of that name which he wrote and presented, brought Don Cupitt into our homes, and gave prominence to a movement which was gathering momentum at that time, rightly so, towards the building of bridges between the various faiths of the world.

In France Martin spoke of his mother as follows:

> She was a lifelong learner and encouraged us to be likewise. To be a lifelong learner she had to remain open-minded.

Her Times obituary details the formidable variety of contexts in which Rosemarie shared her enthusiasm for, and growing expertise in, comparative religion. To do this within an enclosed academic environment, such as a university theology faculty, is one thing - easy, you may say. To do so outside of academe, among (in her best sense) ordinary people is something else entirely, and very enterprising.

During the 1970s and, especially, the 1980s, the College of Adult Education in Manchester was a beleaguered institution, caught in the ideological cross-fire between Thatcher's central government on the one side and an extremely hard-line local government on the other. Funding was always tight, and we seemed constantly to be looking over our shoulder for threats to our very existence - fears which, all too soon, proved founded with the College's closure as an independent institution in 1990.

Before then, though, some brave and visionary Principals, notably Ronnie Wilson and William Tyler, encouraged their staff tutors to offer a varied and imaginative range of courses. The main teaching burden fell on an army of part-time tutors; and Rosemarie's evening classes comparative religion represent easily one of the most important. Within the increasingly multi-ethnic, multi-faith community which the city of Manchester comprises, her teaching of comparative religion might have seemed obvious; in practice I'm not sure that this was so, particularly as students, especially venturing into near-central Manchester at night, notoriously vote with their feet. The fact that Rosemarie sustained a successful, well-supported and invaluable class over several years speaks volumes for her enthusiasm, her dedication, and her achievements as a teacher in interacting with her devoted adult students. The College closed twenty year ago, Rosemarie's earthly life closed a few weeks ago, but I have no doubt that the importance of her teaching, in the College of Adult Education and elsewhere, will live on in the hearts and minds of those who were lucky enough to have been inspired by her.

Ann Clifton (a colleague at the European School in Brussels)

Just a few memories of working with Rosemarie, and also of seeing her after that. I think that we thought that we were at the beginning of a great project. Our time together dates back to 1974, the early days of British entry to what was then the European Community and here were we, in what we thought was a very fortunate position to have the chance of teaching in this unusual and unique establishment at the time. The school had something like 3,200 students, teachers I think were about 250 and there were more than 50 teachers who were involved with teaching religion or some kind of mild formation. So this was a very different experience from the schools we had come from in the UK. I only had a small number of hours compared with Rosemarie, so we would meet like ships in the night, but she was always there ready with support and advice, she had more experience than I had.

As was said yesterday evening Rosemarie touched the lives of every person she came in contact with. I think she was driven in the best sense of the word, she was kind, she was compassionate she was very very interested in the lives and the wellbeing of the students with whom she came in contact and she believed in the goodness of everybody that she met.

We shared something else as well, that was having, what the Belgians would call them, la famille - we each had 4 children and although Rosemarie's children were not with her I actually felt that I knew Martin, Philip, Crispin and Rebecca because she talked about them so much and she loved them so very very deeply.

So she was there always if you like to give me advice with my younger set of four boys and shared experiences with me of the joys and challenges of teenage years and generally in bringing up children. What I found very touching yesterday and today was to look at the four children and see in them Rosemarie, be it in features, in mannerisms, or just something there and that very much brought her back to me because I haven't seen her for some time.

She gave me some interesting advice about buying a house in France. I think I'm right in that it was Martin and Crispin, who she explained to me, went off looking around various parts of the French countryside looking for "A Vendre" signs and that was the thing to do - not go look in the *Sunday Times* or property newspapers but to do it all on foot. We were then very fortunate to go and stay in Vigneau and to use a common word, I was gobsmacked by this fantastic place, which I felt, was almost large enough to fit a battalion in.

When we eventually got around to purchasing a place ourselves I have to say it was on a much more modest scale, referred to as Ann's shack. It's very nice to know that Vigneau has continued in the Wedell family.

Last of all, through George I would like to thank her and George for two very special events, that to me were very special events. I come from Wythenshawe and Rosemarie knew that my heart, shall I say, was partly still in Manchester, so she invited Peter and myself to two lovely events. The first event was a visit, probably a British Council organised visit, by the Royal Exchange Theatre

Company who performed a Winter's Tale in one of the Brussels theatres. Then I think through Rosemarie I was able to get one of actors to come and talk to a particular group of students in the school. I think there were probably concerns by their parents about a new ambition to enter the world of theatre. The second was the European officer, now I'm not sure if it was the Commission started having European officers from regions in order to talk about investment. This was either the officer for Manchester or the Northwest and again we were invited to what turned out to be a very splendid evening.

I am still a great believer in the Europe project. I know that I am in very good company here and I know Rosemarie would agree, actually we do hang out a flag occasionally in our small Oxfordshire village; they probably think we are stark raving mad. However, we do it on Europe day which is usually around May 8th. Rosemarie it was a privilege to know you. Thank you for your friendship and may you rest in peace.

Sheila Cooper (a student of the University of the Third Age)

The University of The Third Age is a worldwide organisation founded to give opportunities to retired people to learn together to participate in joint activities and socialise and it is run on a group basis.

Rosemarie was contacted by the Stockport branch in September 1987 and offered to start a group on comparative religion. This began in the December of the same year. She travelled cheerfully in all weathers from Didsbury to the Dialstone Centre on Monday mornings to start at 10am. She was very popular with the Group members, bright and interested in each member of the group, always patient in answering our questions. It was evident that her real desire was to pass on her knowledge of world religions and of life in other countries.

The members were a mixed bag, Roman Catholic, Church of England, Methodists, Baptists, Quakers, Humanists and agnostics, all eager to learn and Rosemarie fulfilled that need with much expertise and sensitivity. She consulted us about what she was to deliver next and turned up to the next meeting with her fully researched notes books and slides to illustrate her lectures and there were several members who were inspired to read these books at home. At about 11.15 we adjourned to the cafe for coffee and I remember many a discussion continuing with laughter and friendly arguments over the drinks, so involved were we in the topic of the day.

One member later wrote that the key words to the way Rosemarie's classes have evolved and held together so well over the years were sharing commitment and fellowship. She herself always maintained how much she gained from the group and the comradeship of those ten years. Another wrote I feel privileged to have listened for over ten years of Rosemarie's talks we covered Christianity, Judaism, Islam, Hinduism, Buddhism and even Zoroastrianism. All this gave us an historic overview of the similarities and differences of the various faiths in our world today. The presentations were aimed at revealing the best of each faith and where possible Rosemarie tried to show the variations within a religion. This illustrated the richness and complexity of human thought and beliefs. That richness really revealed itself in the last of our sessions where we questioned Rosemarie or interacted with each other. All these stimulations totalled a wonderful learning experienced.

I personally consider myself very fortunate to have had the opportunity to meet Rosemarie and benefit from her knowledge, sensitivity and understanding. She was made an honorary life member of the Stockport UTA and I know this gave her great pleasure. We all missed her so much when she retired but remember her with great affection.

Rosemarie and Civil Society

Pauline Morris (the wife of Charles, a member of Harold Wilson's Government; and the mother of Estelle, a member of Tony Blair's Government)

I do feel honoured at being asked to make a contribution to this memorial service for Rosemarie and I am grateful to George and the family for inviting me to do so. I am probably not alone today in learning something new about Rosemarie which I didn't know before. Apart from her family, all of us met her and knew her in different situations. Our respect and love was there for an exceptional woman.

Life's journey is individual to each one of us, but Rosemarie's life was fascinating in the contrasts which it embraced. Her early life in Germany, her move to England and her pioneering work with young people and religion all mark her out as having quite an extraordinary life.

She understood that working with children and young people; you can shape and influence the future. Equally, she knew that religion is the force for good and unity but only if it is underpinned with tolerance. Her pioneering work showed both her understanding of human nature and her desire to share with others what she had learnt through her own life experience. She was of course also one of that generation of women who broke through so many barriers making it easier for others to follow.

The story of her life is indeed remarkable but in a way that isn't the thing I remember most about her. Charles and I met Rosemarie and George in the early 70s and years of friendship have followed. I have lost count of the number of occasions I have spent in their home catching up on family news, sharing views and opinions and of course putting the world to right. When I look back now I realise that Rosemarie always had something new to say, but in many ways she was always the same. She was always calm, warm, patient and interesting and for me that is what made her a special person. Those very personal qualities made her a good listener, a wonderful advocate for her beliefs and a real friend to so very many of us.

Rosemarie and I had a very different life journey but something always linked us, it was a picture that hung on their wall at their home. It was a school in Miles Platting, an area in the city of Manchester. I attended that school back in the thirties. I was a pupil and Rosemarie eventually worked there as a teacher. Our connection at the school was very different but Rosemarie and I had the ability to empathise and relate to the people in such a way that we could talk about it as if we had grown up there together.

Rosemarie has been a part of mine and Charles' life for four decades. She was a good friend and her not being here does leave a void. Each one of us has our own memories. I have always admired Rosemarie for her professional courage, her determination, her ability and her skills. But it is as a friend that I will remember her most, as a warm and generous person and for the home she and George created in Cranmer Road where, like me, so many others here today knew we were always welcome.

David Sandiford (A Liberal Democrat Councillor & former Lord Mayor of Manchester)

Rosemarie was a member of the Liberal Party and then the Liberal Democrats for many years up to her death and, with George, was a generous supporter and enthusiast for the Party.

She was a member of the local Party in Withington ward, one of the most successful wards in the city of Manchester in the late 70s. Later, after boundary changes, Cranmer Road moved into Didsbury East ward. It so happened that I represented both wards in turn and so that kept me in contact with Rosemarie. When I was Lord Mayor of Manchester it gave me great pleasure to accept one of Rosemarie's personal invitations to attend one of her fundraising concerts. I decided I should accept as Lord Mayor and so was able to attend the concert in Cranmer Road in the Lord Mayor' chains when I was able at the end of the music to thank Rosemarie for her thoughtfulness and generosity in helping so many charities over the years.

Rosemarie was a strong supporter and active encourager of women and ethnic minorities in the Party though she never herself sought to stand for public office.

The very first time that I met Rosemarie in Liberal politics was when she was accompanying George as the Liberal candidate in the June Euro-election of 1979 (I had just been elected a city councillor for Withington Ward in May). George also stood in the Euro-election of 1984; in those days, we still had first past the post elections in single member constituencies and George, frankly, never stood a realistic chance of winning as a candidate for the then 3rd Party.

However, it was important to fly the flag and to have a good time if possible. I especially remember an open-topped bus with George and Rosemarie on board touring Manchester city centre with loud hailers and lots of balloons.

On board we had a slightly notorious American pop star of the day by the name of PJ Proby wearing rather tight leather trousers and singing some of his latest releases who managed to get it slightly wrong when he asked the crowds to support someone he referred to as "George Weedle", much to the delight of my very young daughters who were getting into the spirit of things. Rosemarie of course was fazed by nothing.

I googled PJ Proby yesterday and amazingly I discovered that he is touring England at this moment at the age of 73 and actually appeared at the Bridgewater Hall in Manchester just this last Thursday, and will be appearing in a show in Manchester in January. Perhaps, George, we should pay him a visit for old times' sake.

Rosemarie was, of course, very much an internationalist and was happy in a Party that was in the same mould. Her book, *Halfway Round the World*, her diaries of her visits to China, India, and Africa, not only show this but gave me a good insight into her thinking and her generosity of spirit. She could also surprise me in the book with her outspokenness.

Her friends in the Party will miss her.

Bryan Saunders (A senior Civil Servant & Convener of the Chantry Group)

When I first met the Wedells they were living at the Chantry in Sevenoaks. It must have been very early in the 1950s and Martin was a baby. When I next met them they were living in a flat in Belgravia. It was not the stratospheric property location it is now, but they had a first floor flat in a lovely Georgian house. Eberhard was an Assistant Principal in the Ministry of Education and they had started as they meant to go on by inviting a group of friends to a coffee evening to discuss issues of the day in politics, economics, the arts and anything else that makes humans human. As I remember it, there was a carpet on the floor, but a lot of bare boards and just enough chairs for everyone to sit down. None of this mattered. The coffee was excellent and the conversation invariably high-minded.

Eberhard soon moved on to the Social Affairs department of the Church of England, where they first thought him a great catch but then found it was they who were caught in a vision for which they were not prepared. He left for the Independent Television Authority. Meanwhile, the family home had moved to more commodious quarters in less exalted terraces overlooking Battersea Park, where I remember Rosemarie's calm maternal presence spreading warmth and comfort not only over the family, but also all their many friends.

Inevitably time spread us far and wide and monthly coffee evenings eventually became no longer possible. The Chantry Group, though we did not find it necessary to give it a name until the 1990, had to find other ways to meet and a day or two at a weekend gradually emerged as the comfortable format. Thus it still continues and I am pleased to see several of its present members here today. The high-minded eclecticism continues, but that is not he main value we find in it. Those of us who do not always find it easy to maintain the moral and intellectual altitude nevertheless never fail to find a warm and friendly welcome Rosemarie was always interested in us, in what we were doing and thinking, however outlandish it might be. Friendship is the quality for which I will always remember her. What I want to say for Rosemarie today can be summed up in two words: Thank you.

Rosemarie the Pilgrim

The Revd Dr Marcus Braybrook (President of the World Congress of Faiths)

It is a privilege to be asked to share in this thanksgiving for the life of Rosemarie

Wedell. I join with others in assuring George and the family of Mary's and my deep sympathy and also bring good wishes from those members of the World Congress of Faiths who knew Rosemarie. I also wish to voice my personal appreciation of Rosemarie's constant support and encouragement for my interfaith work, especially in those days when religious authorities looked on with disapproval. My only sadness is that I saw less of her than I would have wished.

Rosemarie herself made a distinguished contribution to the teaching of world religions. But she was one who, in the words of the distinguished Japanese Buddhist scholar Masao Abe, moved from 'mutual appreciation' to 'mutual transformation'. Grateful for the inspiration of the faith community, which has nourished us, our spiritual journey is enriched by the wisdom and writings of many spiritual traditions.

For Sir Francis Younghusband, who founded the World Congress of Faiths to which Rosemarie belonged, the fellowship of faiths was much more than the search for good community relations.

"The ultimate aim of the Fellowship." Younghusband said, "can only be to intensify our sense of kinship with the universe to the mystic degree - to that point when the individual feels as if he or she were in love with all people and all living beings."

Rosemarie was thankful for all the contemporary signs that, despite the newspaper headlines, we are moving in the words of Wayne Teasdale, a pioneer of inter-spirituality, to a 'rebirth of the human community that will harmonise itself with the cosmos and finally make peace with all beings.'

For Rosemarie, I trust, that peace is now a reality and that the Sea of Faith has become an Ocean of Love.

Dr Valerie Clark (A member of the Sea of Faith Network)'

Rosemarie and I were both members of the Sea of Faith network, a group whose statement of intent is "exploring and promoting religious faith as a human creation." The network and the conferences arose from a book called *The Sea of Faith* by Don Cupitt, then Dean of Emmanuel College Cambridge, published in 1984 and Rosemarie was involved with the network from the early days. A television programme based upon the book came later. *Sea of faith* is a phrase from Matthew Arnold's poem *Dover Beach* in which the decline of religion is likened to the tide's melancholy retreat from the shore.

I first remember Rosemarie at Sea of Faith conferences in the early 1990s, sitting in the front row, listening intently to the speakers and often sharply questioning them. She was trying to get at the meaning of words in order to find new concepts within them. What I will share with you now is my recognition of her ongoing quest to find new meanings for herself and other people within language, experience and personal and world history.

In 1991 in a letter in the Sea of Faith magazine she explored the idea of the "Christian language without (as she called it) an endless body of adjectives like divine, eternal, supernatural etc attached to nouns like God, Eternity, heaven etc" She said that if we got rid of the adjectives, tile nouns would have to go too - leading to a more mature Christianity.

In 1993 she was talking and writing about the need for people to make themselves and their societies more truly human. This, she said, would involve a period of re-education and looking back at strands in the history of human society that illuminated the darkness and hopelessness of the human condition.

Such searching (she said) would find practical examples of holiness and goodness at work in the midst of apparently insurmountable human depravity, squalor and apathy - whereby this current generation could read and learn anew from human history.

By 1997 she had written a paper on her own spiritual development that she circulated to many people. Part of it, published in the Sea of Faith magazine, spoke of her current awareness of her place within the cosmos:

"I am learning to see myself as a psycho-physical organism among countless sentient and human organisms, living in the biosphere and as part of the ecosystem of this beautiful planet Earth, with the potential for psycho-mystical awareness in my relationships with nature, the universe and my fellow human beings."

Looking back at her experiences of life so far seemed to have given her hope and pleasure for the future. She said she was "(a) in a state of wonder about the range of the human imagination and its rational mind, world-wide; (b) in a state of thankfulness that human beings have evolved and are still evolving towards greater 'complex consciousness' and personal autonomy; and (c) are more willing to take on responsibility for their natural, social, economic and political , environment."

Somewhat provocatively - but, I think, quite honestly - she said she would like to change the Sea of Faith's statement of intent in light of her thinking and development, by omitting the phrase "religious faith" completely and calling it instead "A network for exploring and promoting the human potential for creating human values," I think Rosemarie continued to rethink and replicase her place in - and relationship with - the world, its inhabitants and their values throughout her whole life. I shall miss her and, like many other groups that she belonged to, The Sea of Faiths will miss her contribution also.

Dr Christiaan Vonck (the Director of the Faculty for the Comparative Study of Religions, in association with the Free University of Brussels)

Already in the 70s we had contact with Rosemarie Wedell, born Rosemarie Winckler.

We were advised by Rosemarie to get in contact with the Revd Marcus Braybrooke and in those years a Belgian Branch of World Congress of Faiths was organised.

The result was the founding and the recognition of a University level Faculty for comparative Study of Religion, a Faculty which believed that teaching religion and other ideologies is best achieved when it is done by those committed to them.

Rosemarie was not only a founding member; she gave us a layout for the first Academic year 1980-81, life is interesting and full of surprises. Thanks to Rosemarie contact was made with the Spalding Trust in the UK. We still needed funds in order to enlarge a dream for a better world. A better world starts with education. In our Faculty (FVGT) we agree that we disagree. We do not compare religions: Students do.

One day I received a phone call from Mr Wedel. Not 'our' George Wedell. Yes, it happened that the Consul-General of Germany in Antwerp keeps the same name as you, dear George! Because of this fact the Embassy of Germany in Brussels started to assist the FVG with books, documents and some funds - of course all related to the agreements between Germany and Belgium.

Yes, our main link with the UK was Rosemarie. I hope the link UK with Belgium will remain strong and solid. That also was her wish. Her last 'move' was in December 2009 when she signed a document for the Belgian Government concerning the accreditation of our new diplomas.

Now, many a time we say: people come and go. I do not believe that. Bodies come and go. Rosemarie's body did pass away. Forever her actions, her deeds and her teachings shall live. As fresh as the green grass of paradise.

Ridwanya Abdullah (widow of Imam Khurshed Abdullah and a long time Muslim friend of Rosemarie's)

Rosemarie and I met many years ago when I first married my Muslim husband. She was the first person to welcome us into her home. Since then we have had a great deal of love and friendship between us. So all I have to say really today is that I loved her, she was a great person and a wonderful Christian; and I hope that what she has brought to all of us will benefit us for the rest of our lives. Thank you very much for listening.

Rosemarie's vision of a World Society

These extracts from a chapter contributed by her to a volume entitled *No Discouragement* [4] were read by **Thomas Wedell**, her grandson.

My encounters with the other world-views have convinced me of the need for a new, value-system in our European Region. Europeans are still living in a state of dualism and tension after almost two thousand years, the dualism between the spirit and the body, between religion and science, and between supernatural Reality and the phenomenal environment of our Earth and Universe. They have made me realise that they are as much concerned with the discovery of meaning and value for human life and behaviour as we are.

As my friends in the global network of the Interfaith Movement and I look towards the 21st century, we envisage that the emerging European Christian Humanism will be matched and complemented by the humanism of other faith communities and human societies. Together they will contribute to the creation of a world society where the conditions of peace, justice and order between and within nations and societies can prevail.

[4] *No Discouragement: Exploring Faith in the Chantry Group* London, Avon Books 1997 p 248-262.

The *Pilgrim's Song* by John Bunyan (1684) and Others
    The gathering ended with the singing of *He who would valiant be*

He who would valiant be
'gainst all disaster,
Let him in constancy
Follow the Master.
There's no discouragement shall
Make him once relent
His first avowed intent
To be a pilgrim.

Who so beset him round
With dismal stories
Do but themselves confound
His strength the more is.
No foes shall stay his might;
Though he with giants fight,

He will make good his right
To be a pilgrim.

Since, Lord, Thou dost defend
Us with thy Spirit,
We know we at the end,
Shall life inherit.
Then fancies flee away
'I'll fear not what men say,
I'll labor night and day
To be a pilgrim.

MUSIC

1980 Rosemarie launched some musical evenings in aid of causes which she regarded as important. They have continued over the years with Crispin and David Morgan as the musicians, reinforced from time to time by one or other of their musical friends.

The next musical evening was planned in July for November. Since Rosemarie's death we have decided to include elements of the musical performance in our commemoration of her life and we welcome those who normally come to these evenings.

David Morgan (piano), Rebecca Wedell (Mezzo-Soprano)
& Crispin Wedell (Clarinet)
Felix Mendelssohn: Sonata for Clarinet & Piano
(2nd Movement)
Franz Schubert/F von Schober: An die Musik
Gabriel Fauré: Après un Rève

You Gracious Art, in many dismal hours
Where I have been bound by life's unruly course,
You have kindled a warm love in my heart
And carried me to a better world,

To a better world
Oft comes a sigh, a holy chord from your harp
A glimpse of heaven and the sight of better times before me.
I thank you for this, you gracious Art
You gracious Art, my thanks to you.

Angela Youngman Stewart (Mezzo-Soprano),
Rosemary Robinson (Piano), David Morgan, (Piano)
Chanya Ambalu-Wedell (Violin)

George Herbert/Alexander Youngman
Love Bade Me Welcome
Giuseppe Tartini Sonatina movements 1 & 2
Two German Songs
(Heinrich Barmann) Adagio

LOVE bade me welcome; yet my soul drew back,
Guilty of dust and sin.
But quick-eyed Love, observing me grow slack
From my first entrance in,
Drew nearer to me, sweetly questioning
If I lack'd anything.

'A guest,' I answer'd, 'worthy to be here:'
Love said, 'You shall be he.'
'I, the unkind, ungrateful? Ah, my dear,
I cannot look on Thee.'
Love took my hand and smiling did reply,
'Who made the eyes but I?'

'Truth, Lord; but I have marr'd them: let my shame.
Go where it doth deserve.'
'And know you not: says Love, 'Who bore the blame?'
'My dear, then I will serve.'
'You must sit down,' says Love, 'and taste my meat.'
So I did sit and eat.

David Morgan (piano), Rebecca Wedell (Mezzo-Soprano)
& Crispin Wedell (Clarinet)
Franz Schubert/Leopold zu Stollberg Auf dem
Wasser zu Singen
Frederic Chopin's Etude Op. 10 No.3.

Camille Saint-Saens: The Swan

The Soul's Farewell (a prose translation)

In the midst of shimmering waves the boat glides like a swan
Ah, with the joy of shimmering waves, so too glides the soul.
From heaven down to the waves the evening light dances around the boat

Over the top of the grove in the west the sunset waves to us
Below the branches of the trees in the east, the reeds rustle,
In heavenly joy and the peace of the woods the soul breathes in the sunset's glow

Ah, time disappears before me on the frothing crests of rippling waves.
Just as yesterday and today, time will disappear tomorrow on shimmering wings
Until I myself, high upon radiant wings, disappear on the current of time.

The 2011 letter

THE CHRISTMAS LETTER reflects a reorganisation of the household without Rosemarie. She contributed substantially to the reflective pieces of the letter, and they will not be the same without her. Having completed a half-century of them we shall see whether the recalling of those years will be of continuing interest to our contemporaries.

19 Cranmer Road,
Didsbury
Manchester 20

Advent 2011

We send Christmas greetings this year without Rosemarie's contribution. Of the 48 letters written at Christmas over the 50 years since 1962 we seem to have missed only 1963 and 1967, and I cannot remember why. Rosemarie used to write much of them in the early years. I think we wanted to let our friends, who were mainly in the south of the country, know what we were doing in Manchester. I suppose it was curious that a family that was well settled in the Metropolis should chose to move north.

In so far as my jobs were concerned they were national in scope. In the Ministry of Education we were at the decision-making centre. The local education authorities were at our beck and call. It was our job to think and plan better than they could, and to make sure that our views of education were more intelligent and forward thinking than theirs. At the Board for Social Responsibility we were new and innovative compared with most dioceses, and with the Church Assembly were at the hub of the decision making process. In the Independent Television Authority we were designing an entirely new system. It was one decision to go for regional devolution. We were concerned to encourage local initiative in so far as the economics of the system allowed.

It was my concern at that time to give local communities more of a chance and to see how far they could do better for themselves that made me move to Manchester even though my salary as a professor was less than my salary as the secretary of the ITA. I was also hoping to have more time and more freedom to follow my hunches. In the event that was so. As a family we became more aware of the strength of regional traditions and values in the North West., we also learnt to know Europe beyond our shores. For the children moving around the world Europe became their back yard. We tried to enable them to become at least trilingual in English, French and German. In the event Martin, Crispin and Philip achieved Russian, Swahili, Urdu and Mandarin, among others.

As far as 2011 is concerned, our year has been spent largely on the effort to reorganise our lives without Rosemarie. We have commemorated her life by scattering her ashes on the Tertre at Vigneau and in the rose garden at Cranmer Road. Her studio has been well used by overnight visitors and by EG as the rest of the house has been taken over by the grandchildren. And the re-discovery of these Christmas letters, in all of which Rosemarie has recounted her doings and thinking recalls her existential influence on all our lives.

In the meantime Martin, Crispin and Philip, Rebecca and I send our warmest good wishes for Christmas 2011.